EIGHT BEGIN

EIGHT BEGIN

ARTISTS' MEMORIES OF STARTING OUT

Ronald Bladen
Lois Dodd
Sally Hazelet Drummond
Al Held
Alex Katz
William King
Philip Pearlstein
George Sugarman

Edited by Ada Katz

These eight pieces began as interviews and were edited into mono-logues with the voices of the artists intact.

The artists included are Alex Katz, Lois Dodd, William King, Sally Hazelet Drummond, Al Held, Ronald Bladen, George Sugarman, and Philip Pearlstein, interviewed in that sequence, at the artists' conve-nience.

They came to Manhattan by chance or to go to art school after World War Two. They all remained by choice, finding an emotional, intellec-tual, and social life in "downtown" New York into which they seemed to fit.

With exception of two, Ronald Bladen and George Sugarman, they are of the same age group. They are all, however, of the same artistic generation. They were all founders or early members of cooperative art galleries of the early 1950s on 10th Street. The galleries came to be known collectively as "10th Street." This is where the stories end and where their professional lives begin.

— Ada Katz, 1975

"... some really sad news is the announcement of its last season by the Tanager Gallery. This artists' cooperative gallery has been the most distinguished in the 10th Street area for several years, one where each year at Christmastime its invitational exhibition showed small works by the most illustrious names in contemporary American painting alongside lesser or totally unknown ones to the benefit of all; these were big shows hung with extraordinary taste and discernment. At other times of the year the Tanager has given one-man shows to a roster of artists any uptown gallery would be proud to boast, and indeed many of the artists have moved up there . . . The member artists who have struggled through the vicissitudes of keeping a gallery open for ten years may not get their just reward, but they should get a lot of praise and gratitude. The Tanager, through the high quality of its exhibitions over the years, and through the fact that its exhibitions were chosen by a group of artists with little or no possibility of, let alone interest in, commercial values, was able to confer on a first show by an unknown artist a distinction pretty much unavailable to the younger artist elsewhere."

—Frank O'Hara, "Art Chronicle" II, *Kulchur* 6, summer 1962

CONTENTS

13   Introduction

16   Ronald Bladen

22   Lois Dodd

32   Sally Hazelet Drummond

42   Al Held

68   Alex Katz

78   William King

88   Philip Pearlstein

102   George Sugarman

113   Afterword

Introduction

In 1974 Ada Katz began a project to interview artists associated with the downtown New York collectives that became known as the 10th Street galleries. Over the course of a year, she interviewed Ronald Bladen, Lois Dodd, Sally Hazelet[1], Al Held, Alex Katz, William King, Philip Pearlstein, and George Sugarman. Katz conceived of her interviews as conversations in the artists' studios (their homes) and posed questions to her subjects that sought to uncover who they were before they were artists: Where did they come from? Who were they as children? What were their families like? And ultimately, how did they begin as artists?

As Katz transcribed the tape-recorded interviews, she removed her questions, leaving only the voices of the artists. Yet the intimacy and candor of the remaining narratives reveal her gifts as an interlocutor and listener. She created a relaxed space for her subjects to tell their stories, and what resulted is a series of frank reflections on origins. While these eight artists come from distinct backgrounds and are stylistically and temperamentally diverse, their accounts share a common thread of deliberation: how they became artists at a time when this path was not at all clear.

The 10th Street galleries were cooperative ventures that operated as alternatives to the more established, commercially viable uptown galleries on Madison Avenue and Fifty-seventh Street. Located on East 10th Street between Third and Fourth Avenues, they were fully artist-run, with members painting walls, selecting and hanging works of art, and taking turns as gallery attendants. The Tanager Gallery at 90 East 10th Street was one of the first of these enterprises. Founded in 1952 by Charles Cajori, Lois Dodd, Angelo Ippolito, William King, and Fred Mitchell, the collective also included Sally Hazelet, Alex Katz, and Philip Pearlstein and operated for a decade before closing in 1962. Ronald Bladen, Al Held, and George Sugarman, the other artists whom Katz interviewed, were founding members of the Brata Gallery at 56 Third Avenue, another fixture on the 10th Street scene from 1957 to the mid-1960s.

Katz's interviews capture a moment that seems remote in to-

---

1   Sally Hazelet married Frank (Wick) Drummond in 1962 and changed her name at that time to Sally Hazelet Drummond.

day's world of mega galleries and multimillion-dollar art deals. These artists lived and worked without the promise of commercial success. Instead, they created an environment that fostered artistic ambition and provided a sense of kinship that they craved. Significantly, they established their own venues, which provided alternatives to the growing hegemony of the Abstract Expressionists and their followers. The supportive environment on 10th Street allowed artists with a contrarian tendency to flourish, and the primacy of the downtown scene for all eight artists is clear in these interviews. This was a circle of colleagues and friends who banded together for intellectual, creative, and social exchange; they established a sense of community and believed that together they could make their lives as artists. Four decades later, the significance of these artists to contemporary art shows just how successful they were in achieving their goals.

Sharon Corwin
Carolyn Muzzy Director and Chief Curator
Colby College Museum of Art

Ronald Bladen, c. 1965-68

RONALD BLADEN

December 12, 1974

I was born in Vancouver, British Columbia, in the west of Canada. My mother and father are English, from towns near London, maybe two hours away. They came to this continent just before the First World War. They came across, and they settled in Vancouver. It was strange because they met in Vancouver. Their families had known each other, but they had never met before. I have the feeling they went to Vancouver because it was the thing to do at that time. There were a number of people coming out, and my father met a number of people on the boat coming over who later became cronies. They all went around together for years. My mother and father met in a bohemian circle in Vancouver that was run by a woman who was sort of an extraordinary person. This circle was not so much concerned with the arts as with a style of living.

My father was a metallurgist, and he found it extremely difficult to make a living, so he did many things beside that. Ultimately, he set up a couple of steel mills in the States, and we moved to the States. He was very interested in growing things. He had a greenhouse and was in a number of business ventures. My father, actually, prior to coming out to Vancouver, existed in a small literary circle around Yeats and A.E. Russell in Ireland. That was another life, though. My father's name was Kenneth.

My mother, Muriel Beatrice, had been studying at the Sorbonne in Paris for a few years before she came out, and she was very involved in music and languages. When she was young, she was very involved in the theater. I think she wanted to be an actress.

I came to the States for the first time when I was about four years old. I only stayed until I was in the seventh grade. Then I went back to Canada. Then I stayed in Canada until I was about twenty, I guess, and I came back down. The two countries seemed very different socially. I preferred the United States because there wasn't such an English pall on everything. It was easier for me here than it was there. In school it was more difficult there. They had more strict and rigid learning processes. I found school very difficult.

In the United States, I lived in Washington. I lived, actually, in the same town that Motherwell was born in, Aberdeen, Washington.

Aberdeen about that time, I don't remember it, but it was a center. Grace Harbor was a literary center. I think that D.H. Lawrence published a small literary magazine there. We lived in the country as well as in the city. We lived in the middle of the woods with a roadhouse next door, and my father used to set the tables for the weekend festivities and so on. My mother was studying jazz with the piano player. And every once in a while the police or the internal revenue would come and they'd find a body somewhere way back in the woods and a still. It was sort of sad in a way. They were very nice though, the roadhouse people.

Besides school, I played games. I played a lot of sports. This was when I was around ten years old. I played a lot of baseball, football, and so on. I remember my mother attempted to teach me piano, and it was utterly impossible. It was completely impossible. I think it was the first time she ever gave up on anything. But I'm now completely involved in sound and trying to play. It's very much a part of my life now, regardless of whether it's successful or not. I'm very involved in it, but I was incapable of being taught anything.

I have a lot of my early drawings and paintings. They go back to 1928, and some were dated '27 and some '29. I was encouraged very much by my mother. I did a lot of work, and I also was encouraged by other people, friends of my mother's. I had a one-man show of paintings and watercolors at the University of Oregon when I was ten years old. I remember doing my first social protest work, a drawing, at that time, 1929, entitled *The Strike*. It really was a portrait of my mother with pictures of striking people and distraught people in the background. I was also making copies of Botticelli and da Vinci and Matisse and Picasso and so on. These were not from originals or anything like that, they were from books. I was especially familiar with Botticelli, Titian, Raphael, and Degas.

My parents didn't have paintings in their home, not in the true sense. They had a copy of one minor Old Master that somehow must have come down from their relatives. It was called *The Madonna of the Cat*. Apparently, the original is somewhere in a Boston museum or somewhere like that. It's by a well-known Italian [Federico Barocci, *The Madonna of the Cat* (*La Madonna del Gatto*), 1575, in the collection of The National Gallery, London].

And I had a relation to a number of people arranged by my family, so I was aware of a certain kind of social art that was going on. I think that was a part of the WPA effort, and later on it became a strong kind of social realism. A lusty, earthy kind of thing. In Canada I studied while I was in high school, taking painting lessons privately. I went to this man's studio and I just painted. On occasions we'd go out on sketching trips, on weekends. I was about fifteen at this time, and I met Jack Shadboldt, one of Canada's foremost painters now.

I was involved with art very early. I did it myself, and my mother just encouraged it and encouraged it. She never once prevented it from happening. The same with my father, in a sense, although he was more removed — but there was never an attempt to stop me. My sister, who was younger, was not really a part of my conscious life. Maybe very deeply so, but never on the surface. I was too involved in myself. I was pretty alien in those days. I was pretty hostile, and I didn't talk to anybody. I had all my own friends of course, but I was pretty difficult for my parents when I was an early teenager.

I tried to check back and find out if my family had a history of artistic tendencies, but it's not so. But I did find something out that for me was very interesting, which my mother had never told me — that there were two cousins who played on the All-England cricket team, those very great matches they had with Australia and so on. That would have been very interesting for me when I was there more recently. They were great cricket players. Athletic activities were a natural part of life. I played tennis in a lot of amateur tournaments with people who people here don't remember anymore. But it was important to me only in a very minor way.

I dropped out of high school for two years, and I went to art school in Vancouver and stayed there a year. Then I dropped out for two more years and went to San Francisco to the California School of Fine Arts. The San Francisco school in one way was very different from the Vancouver school, but when I look back, in another way, it really wasn't. At the time it seemed to me more vital, and it had more reason for existence. In the other school, there seemed to be much more emphasis among the students themselves on design and commercial arts rather than fine arts. In San Francisco, at that time, Ed Corbett and Jimmy Weeks were there, and for me it was a very intense and vital time in relation to art, not so much in relation to the instructors as in relation to the other students. This was 1939 to 1942.

I got out of going to WWII. I went to work in the shipyards after I finished up at school. I was rejected from the army. I went to work in the shipyards, and I became involved or had been involved in a large poetry group there. Then I was told to leave the United States, and I had to go through the Canadian Army draft and their labor draft and finally got back down to San Francisco and back to the shipyards.

The poetry group wasn't a group in a formal sense. I happened to know a lot of poets, and they all were sort of revolving around Kenneth Rexroth and Robert Duncan. There wasn't so much activity in painting and sculpture at the time. The activity was literary, and also a little later Ginsberg, Kerouac, and Corso came out there. So it was a very lively, intense scene. Kerouac came out either in the late '40s or early '50s. I think it was the early '50s.

All the incidents which are important in relation to an art experience — and there are so many — revolve around being encouraged, being able to think of yourself as being part of the community of artists. I had one painting show at the Six Gallery, after Robert Duncan had it. Duncan's was called King Ubu, then it became the Six Gallery with people from the school after Still and Rothko. I never met them there. I saw a very early show of Still's at the Museum of Art at San Francisco, and I heard all about them all the time. I was out of the school at that time. The only artist that I had come in contact with was [Douglas] MacAgy. They had a jazz band in school, and MacAgy was drummer. And I met Al Held in a bar called The Cellar. It was a jazz club that some musicians had started in order to have a place to play. It was fantastic music for a long time. Jazz was the culture at that time.

I stayed in San Francisco because I had begun to identify myself very much in terms of being a painter, and it never occurred to me to leave. I was in New York, in 1945 or 1946 for a few months, but I went back. That was at the time when Pollock was just beginning to emerge. I saw a show, at Peggy Guggenheim's Art of This Century. He had a number of drawings and watercolors there. When I was in New York, I lived on the East Side at 152 Avenue C, which was Joshua McClough's apartment while he was at Black Mountain, and it became a whole big drug scene. I didn't get up until 3 or 4 o'clock in the afternoon. I was up all night. I was also drawing. It was incredible. We had such incidents as Jimmy the Greek moving in, setting up housekeeping on the floor. It was just too much of a scene.

I went back to San Francisco, and I got married and stayed there until 1955 or '56. I was painting all the time, and I was working in machine shops. I got married in a machine shop and had three jazz bands. I didn't have that much in the way of shows. One or two things shown or one or two small shows. I had a show at Robert Duncan's apartment once. I had very little to do with museums or anything like that. I was really working primarily on my own. They had their sort of local hierarchy in San Francisco, but this was just prior to the time when they really flourished there. Sonia Gechtoff, Manuel Neri, others, they all flourished after I left. They built a kind of local art community, a painting and sculpture community, whereas before there had been much more emphasis on literature. There still is, I think.

I never thought about making money. My thoughts never went much beyond the fantasy of being a great artist, so I never thought of the practical means of doing things. And there wasn't all that much opportunity either. There was no marketplace. Very few galleries.

In the middle 1950s I came to New York for two reasons. One, personal reasons, and the other was I would continue to paint while I was here. I found a compatible, encouraging group. I received tremendous help from Al [Held], no doubt about that. I met the people he knew, like George Sugarman, and that created an immediate small art family — a community, but small like a family. But that existed for me even when I left San Francisco — I never felt the lack of that there. The difference in New York was the opportunity, and the intensity was great. The ideas were much broader and more exciting, and the dedication was absolute, which it wasn't in other places.

Out of that meeting with Al came a certain kind of use of paint — making one's own paint, supposedly — and so we used to buy pigment and mix it up, and that was fine until I started using it very, very thickly. My paintings got so thick that I had four inches of red, six inches of black. So after that, I started to do some rectangles with linear boards held up by rods. They were painted. They were very simple. I thought of these as having no authority. So I moved toward sculpture, but I never thought of actually being a sculptor.

When I came here, I could see more art than I could see in San Francisco. Plus the fact that art was the primary subject of conversation. And there was much time spent going from each studio to studio. We, in a sense, painted each other's paintings and talked about them and went over it and discussed it. It was very closely knit that way.

Lois Dodd on roof of First Street Studio, New York, 1950s

LOIS DODD

November 5, 1974

I was born in Montclair, New Jersey, on April 22, 1927. There were seven members of the family: father, mother, and five daughters, one of whom died in infancy.

I can remember looking out of the window in summertime and seeing large trees, the front yard, etc. I suppose I remember the summer more. You know, when you get visions of yourself and the house, looking out, it's generally the summertime. My next oldest sister and I — I'm the youngest — slept in a porch with eight windows with eight black window shades, or green, with all the little pinpricks and all the images that you think you see. My other two sisters were older and had their own rooms. It was a very suburban, straight sort of house of which there were a couple more that were similar, next door and down.

I suppose those were early suburbs where they didn't build fifty thousand of them but they built two or three. A man went out and built three houses. There was a pear orchard there originally that they built on, and we had a couple of nice pear trees that went across the back of our yard. And there was still an old house that was the original house with more pear trees. Most of the neighbors commuted to the city. Everybody's father went to town to work except for my father who went to sea. He'd be gone for three months at a time, and when he came back, he'd be back for a month at a time. He'd just be around all of the time then. That's a nice way to live.

The house had, on the ground floor, the living room, the dining room, the kitchen, and a sun porch. On the second floor there was a master bedroom, two smaller bedrooms, and a sun porch, which was this other bedroom that my sister and I had, and then there was an attic above with one finished and one unfinished room. This made enough room for all of us to live in. We had no animals. Since my mother was doing most everything during these three-month periods, enough was enough, and she wasn't going to keep animals besides. But the neighbors had animals, and I guess that took care of the animal situation. We had visiting cats.

I had a big back yard, but the only time we tried growing vegetables was during World War Two when everybody had a Victory Garden. I think I tried to grow something and got potatoes the size of peas. I didn't know from nothing what to do. My father planted green stuff, he wasn't all that keen on flowers. I guess my mother wasn't either. They tended to grow bushes, rhododendron, that sort of thing. I remember the cutting of grass and clipping hedges, that was a big thing. Actually, there was a man who came and cut the grass, and if we learned anything about gardening, it was from him. There was an oak tree, a sassafras tree, there were all kinds of trees and bushes and a currant bush back there, but not a lot of flowers.

The house was white on the bottom and brown on the top, brown stain on the top. I remember painting the house once, myself and my sister, when I was in high school. The neighbors were kind of askance, I remember that. I didn't think of the house as belonging more to either parent — neither was more dominant in the house.

My father did all the maintenance when he was there. He could do it, and he did it. Sometimes he bought stuff for the house, but it was always very strange. And he brought back stuff from Africa. He used to sail to South Africa. I remember he brought back this spotted hide of whatever it was, and it got moths. It got heaved out someplace; my mother didn't have any compunction about getting rid of it. The house was pretty functional. They didn't go in for a lot of decoration, it was pretty plain. Once, he bought a sofa that was made out of some leather-like material that he thought would be indestructible. The idea was that he could wash it all off with a hose, and he'd be happy. But the nicest things we had were some of the tables and chairs that my grandfather made — he was a carpenter. I still have some things he made.

My grandfather's house was nice. It had stained glass windows. Everything in it he built or made. It was much more personal. It was within walking distance of us, next to a railroad track. There was a huge cherry tree in the back and a couple of grape arbors. That was nice. He was my father's father and a Civil War veteran. My father and his father were born in Montclair.

My mother's family came from the country more, northern New Jersey. Vanderhoff was her name, or Vanderhoof, I never got it clear. Margaret. Some of the relatives had thick red hair like Jimmy Schuyler or a Rembrandt painting. They mined zinc in Franklin, New Jersey, where my mother came from. One of her brothers went into the mines and wound up with a lung problem, and he was home. He never worked, as I recall, although he lived to be quite old.

But it was a mining town and my mother's father was a millwright, working for the mining company. He died in 1904. My grandmother's brothers were Civil War veterans. My mother, when she was young, worked in a general store in Franklin. That she had a job in a store was interesting in itself, at that time. She could always add much more rapidly than the rest of us. We'd take home our math, couldn't understand it, but she could always do our work.

We didn't help my mother all that much in the house. I think her attitude was: it takes more time, it's got to be done *now*. And when she got sick and we had to cook — and we could — it was a strange new experience.

She was very plain, with hair in a bun. And she was older than other people's mothers. She was not a young-type mother. She was different than other people's mothers that I knew who were around. She was not a suburban type, which was nice. I just don't think suburbs are the greatest places on earth to be growing up. When I was unhappy as a kid — when I think of it now, I wonder if half of it isn't just the way suburbs are. They've got their own little hard-and-fast set up, and people are always desperately trying to succeed. Most of them worked in New York. It's the kind of life that you don't get in a small town or in a city either, where people are just there. I think there was a lot of boredom there.

I don't think of childhood as a period I would want to go back to, ever. You know, you meet older people — I certainly remember older relatives who would say, "Oh, if only I were a child again." Jesus. I can't think of anything worse than being a child again. And yet, I certainly didn't have a miserable childhood, but still. I think you feel so out of control of your own life when you're a kid that you find dreadful things happening that you can't do anything about. When you grow up, at least whatever happens you can control it a little bit more.

So anyway, my mother was very plain and down to earth and not artistic or anything particularly, and neither was my father. The only kinds of things that he collected were paintings of ships, clipper ships, or he made a ship's model. Of course, he liked to do carpentry or anything connected with that, because that's what his father and brother did. I liked the paintings for the same reasons he liked them and not because they were paintings at all.

My father was always interested in going to sea. He went to the New York State Maritime Academy — which was not a place, it was a ship — when he was very young, I guess when he was twelve. He went through the public school system till maybe eighth grade. A lot of people never went completely through at that time. He then went to the Maritime Academy, which was on a boat called the *Saint Mary's*. It was a sailing ship — it wasn't steam. He went there for two or three years, and when he came out, he was an able-bodied seaman.

He began working, and he eventually got to be a captain, not too many years later. The first few years were on sailing ships, and after that it was steam. He always wanted to do that. The other thing he wanted to do was be a farmer. The earliest trip that I remember him ever mentioning is that he went to Alaska. I think, unless I'm remembering wrong, they sailed all the way around South America. I remember he said the trip to Alaska took several years. They set up some kind of a station, or they took people who were setting up some kind of a station. I don't think he was married at that point yet. It's interesting because Sally's father also went to Alaska. He was doing something else — there must have been a big draw to Alaska then. The trip had to be between 1906 and 1910. It was 1906 when he was going to school — it was before the First World War at any rate.

During the First World War he was transporting troops back and forth to France. He was part of the Naval Reserve, but he was never in the Navy — he was always in the Merchant Marine. At the beginning of the Second World War, he'd gotten very sick, had a brain tumor, and he went to Johns Hopkins hospital. He had it removed. My mother and he died within a year of each other. They both were sick at about the same time. She had cancer. It started with breast cancer, and it was way too late when they finally found it. But he had had his operation, which was before hers. They removed his tumor, and he was fine. They were terrific surgeons at Johns Hopkins, because he was sure he was going to die. And then, my mother did die within that year, and the war was going on or had started, and he decided to go back to sea.

My oldest sister was in her early twenties, she was grown, and so we just stayed there in the house, and he went off to convoy stuff to England. And from England what they did was send convoys to Russia, this particular merchant line. They were simply going through the North Sea, back and forth, from Newcastle-on-Tyne in England to Murmansk, Russia, and back and forth. They didn't come back to New York, and finally, they were torpedoed and sunk. And that was the end of the steamship *Richard Bland*.

We once got a narrative of what happened. The weather was freezing. The lifeboats were crashing as they tried to put them in the water. I think half of the crew actually did get rescued, but the weather was so bad and all. The ships, what did they have? They had one gun on deck against air attacks, but it was submarines with torpedoes. In fact, I think that that merchant ship line didn't exist anymore by the end of the war. It literally was demolished during that time.

My oldest sister stopped work then and stayed home. I was still in high school and so was my sister just a little bit older than me, who was having trouble in school at that point. So Betty stayed home, which delighted her because she hated her job so. My father was well insured so we didn't suddenly have to sell the house and move. And my second oldest sister, June, got married and went to California. So the three of us stayed there until I was going to Cooper Union, and when I graduated from Cooper Union, I was still there. I was commuting all that time. And then, when I married Bill, my two sisters at home decided to move out and get an apartment, which they did. We sold the house to cousins who have lived there ever since.

As far as art went, I can remember my sisters all drew. We'd sit and we'd draw. At school or somewhere they got interested, and they liked to draw, and I'd draw, too. We'd see who could do the best this or that. But the art thing was more from school, really. Because in the public school there in Montclair they did have good art teachers. Really lovely people. They always were very encouraging, and it was the thing I enjoyed the most. It was the only thing I did enjoy.

Kindergarten was terrific. I loved kindergarten. It was a big room, just like a loft. It was a double room. We kids built a house out of orange crates and we could paint to our heart's delight. It was a great kindergarten — it was really fun.

There were no ghastly incidents in the early grades. It was when you got to junior high school and all the girls began changing into young women, and it was over my head. There weren't enough oddballs in junior high school. Junior high school was the worst of all. A total mess somehow. In junior high school, frankly, I can't remember any of the teachers at all.

In high school, I remember I was so goddamned shy and backward I could barely talk to anybody, including this teacher who was terribly nice and interested. But anyway, I had enough sense to take the test for Cooper Union. In the high school, they had a big room with a banana tree under a skylight and two teachers. One was an older woman who was just lovely, the other a student teacher who was going to one of the colleges in New Jersey and was all enthusiastic about everything. She told us a little about what was going on in New York and about American artists.

What did I know? Nothing. In fact, that's how I heard about Cooper Union. She told us where it was and that it was free, and several of us should go and take the test. Otherwise we never would have known the place existed or anything about it, and I certainly had no intention of going to college or art school.

I could see myself going to secretarial school, which is what my sister did. My oldest sister went to secretarial school, which she hated intensely, but she did it anyway, and she worked for years in a job that she hated intensely. The second sister also got a job doing shorthand and typing. She worked in a hospital and then got married.

The sister that was closest to me did odder things. The war was on. She went upstate in New York and joined a group that sent people to help farmers. I don't remember what it was called, and I can't remember how it operated. Then she had jobs in war plants and stuff. But none of them went to college, and no one ever thought in terms of anyone going to college. It just wasn't part of the family "scene," really. So it was just chance that I went to Cooper Union. By then, my parents were dead. I don't know what would have happened if they had been alive, if they would have had something else in mind or a strong view of what I should do in life.

In the summertime we just stayed in Montclair. We had no car.

Nobody in the family drove. But our cousins in Franklin, they had all learned to drive and had cars. One cousin used to come and pick us up and take us up there. That was more countryish, which I used to love. Occasionally, we would go down to the Jersey Shore for maybe a week. The Jersey Shore is okay. It's not like Maine — nothing is like Maine. They had a big boardwalk and dressing rooms. I don't know, I never was really that keen on the Shore. It was beautiful, but I think I'd just as soon have stayed at home. I didn't find it hard to stay home.

We never went to camp. I guess my family, they were of an older generation. They never got into kiddie camps. And I must say, I never wanted to go. That would have been like a punishment if they were sending me to camp. I really would have felt terrible. So I did like to stay at home. But I always thought: Wouldn't it be nice if I could travel around with my father?

When this other girl and I went to take the Cooper Union test, I remember standing in a long line and seeing all these very sophisticated-looking kids from the High School of Music and Art, and figuring, well, okay — so we took the test. We didn't feel disappointed. We didn't feel anything. We just took the thing and waited. It was a completely strange and different experience.

I remember making a child and a cart out of clay — I think that's what they said to make. The test was fun though, the questions where you made all the different choices. It wasn't difficult, it was fun. We went back to Montclair, and I didn't think about it, and we both got in. She moved into the Grace Church and was living there after commuting for a year. What ever became of her, I have no idea.

The thing that was interesting at Cooper Union was it was just at the end of the war. It was 1945, and a lot of G.I.s were going back to school, and they were quite a bit older. The class before ours was low on boys. And there was a bit of the school sorority thing going on when we first got there, which was the one thing, I must say, that put me off going to any colleges at all, because I figured it would be more of the same thing that was going on in high school in Montclair, only more so. Once these G.I.s started coming back to Cooper Union, that all began to disappear very rapidly. It was a much more difficult pace to keep up, because the girls were so much younger. It was a fluke, probably, that I got in there, thinking of it, looking back, and we maybe got in just under the wire, before there were any veterans showing up there. It was probably a lucky, happy accident. The atmosphere was very good.

The first year was a foundation course. You took architecture, you took lettering, you took design, you took drawing, and you took grammar and several other humanities courses. It was really remarkable to me that I immediately found friends. I don't remember having so many friends in Montclair. It was astonishing at Cooper Union to meet so many people that were quite like yourself, to finally figure out what it was you liked. I enjoyed the first year. It was hard, but it was terrific.

In the summer, I got jobs. The summer between high school and Cooper Union, I got a job in a yearbook factory. I had been the editor of the high school yearbook, and I got a job in a yearbook factory in Union City, pasting up photographs. That was fun. I was making money. It's always fun making money. I don't think I ever had a job for a whole summer after that period. One time I was working for a guy in the city who did lettering for paperback book covers. I'd start out commuting to the city to some miserable hot job, and then it would peter out. I never had a decent job after that. I got the cure after going to Cooper Union.

During one summer between terms, we all went to draw at a loft on 14th Street. I can remember who went there: Joe Greenberg, Alex Katz, Bill King, Tom Boutis. We formed it, I'm sure, because getting out of art school for the summer, you think, "How will I ever do any of this again?" All the time you're in school you have your friends, and you kind of support one another. That's good, but suddenly you're out, and how are you going to keep in contact with anybody? The drawing group was also politically inclined, so we were stuck between sending off petitions on this or that and getting some drawing done. We used to get into arguments about that: "Are we going to get some drawing done, or are we going to spend our time solving political problems?" That's what destroyed the group. But upstairs there was the Mandolin Society. I swear, twenty or forty people used to meet there and play the mandolin. They were sensational.

In the second year of Cooper Union, I was determined to be a textile designer. I studied textile design because that seemed like a sensible, practical thing to do. But we did also have painting. In a way, that was a compromise, because I knew I wasn't going to go into advertising art, and textile design was something I liked — and I couldn't see fine art as a way to earn money. We had an exciting teacher, a very avant-garde woman, Ruth Reeves, who was teaching textile design. Half the people in the class went into textile design and have done very well. I tried. My friend Shirley Simmons and I tried to do freelance textile designs for a while. We tramped all over town with our designs. We actually sold a few, but we found that the best place to start was at the top. Or otherwise, you'd better start at the bottom and learn all the factory processes and go at it from that end, which is boring, tedious, eye-ruining work. Shirley got a lot of freelance work. She was doing color separations at home on silk screens for textile patterns. She did keep doing it, actually, but I wasn't interested in that.

My painting teacher in the second year was Byron Thomas. His was a terrific course. We made paint, oils, gouache, egg tempera — we did it from that end. We started by making paint first and trying each method out. It was really fun and very good if you're beginning and don't know anything at all. I don't know if I had ever painted with oil paint before. Maybe my sister had a set. You learned in a very down-to-earth way what the materials were, and he used to demonstrate in the class. There would be a model and he'd do a painting. And that was kind of nice, too. That's probably what I should do in my classes, now. You could then take it or leave it. He never in any way tried to impose a style on you. And I never really knew what his painting was like for years. Then I saw his work at the Whitney one time. It was quite different from what I had expected.

I had Peter Busa for design first, then I had Carol Harrison. Busa was not quite in the same range with the others in the design department. There was a very professional design thing going on in the classes, the first and the second year. It was terrific, but you were also kind of terrorized. Well, I was. There was a right, and there was a wrong. And you learned, you did learn, all right. Peter Busa wasn't quite that rigid, and I enjoyed his class for that reason. There was never really anyone there cracking the whip, but there was an atmosphere that made you work hard.

The look, the Cooper Union look, came out of the design classes. There was a kind of style, and if you'd gone into any of the exhibits that took place in those years, you would have recognized it. It was Picassoesque, and the paintings had a lot of design quality in them. You wouldn't have had someone like Bonnard in Cooper Union, because there is no obvious design in Bonnard. He's much more out of an intuitive kind of thing, more individual.

Color was part of the design course, and the main thing about it was that you learned to mix color, you didn't just dab it on out of the tube. I know what the teacher was thinking about in doing that. The impulse for beginners is to squeeze out the paint and use the colors directly. No one thinks about mixing anything, so you have to impose mixing on them, so they will work at it. We were mixing to the point where . . . I remember Jean [Cohen], she was dying to put some red on. Mixing everything made mud, but it had to be beautiful mud. The thing is, if you were trying to use a strong color, you wouldn't have found out how. It was all very tasteful. It was hard, it wasn't easy. It was all brand new. I learned a lot, and we began to go to the Museum of Modern Art.

The third year, we were beginning to wrap it all up. I don't remember who I studied painting with, but it wasn't Morris Kantor, who was there at the time and very well known and important to everybody at Cooper. Nicholas Marsicano had just come, but I didn't have him. Tully Filmus taught drawing. All we actually had was one year of drawing, and then we didn't draw again — not in a classroom situation, at any rate. We drew each other all the time. We used to meet and go down to the waterfront and different places with drawing in mind. In that way the students did have some initiative, and I don't remember that we sat around waiting for the teacher to come to start working, which students seem to do now. They wait until the class begins, and then everything starts. We were always busily working on each other or whatever it was. All the teachers at Cooper Union had the quality of encouragement, which was very important to us all.

The summer after Cooper Union, I was in Montclair. Bill King went to Skowhegan, and in September we were married. And then we went to Rome. Bill had a Fulbright. We spent a year in Rome. We spent some time traveling around, saw all the museums and everything there was to see, and we were working, too. I was painting, and Bill was doing small sculptures.

He enrolled in the Accademia in Rome. You had to enroll in some school. I think that was part of the grant requirement. But when he got there, the sculpture instructor was very opinionated and chopped the legs off his wax figure. And that was the last time he went to the Accademia. He worked out an arrangement, whatever it was, so the school could get paid, and he just worked by himself in wax.

I remember buying little wooden panels to paint on and using egg tempera, not a lot, some. There were other Americans around. Angelo Ippolito was there. Fred Mitchell was there. Bill White was there. And Nancy Rudolph, who was not a painter. She was working at the American Embassy. The Marshall Plan was going on, and she was connected, doing work at the Embassy on that. Then we got connected with a few Italian artists. We all ate in this one place where all the arty types ate. It was Peppino's. It was a *prezzo fisso* place. All the characters went there. There were two places like that. They were both between the Piazza di Spagna and the Piazza del Popolo.

At first we stayed in a *pensione*. We were in a back room freezing to death because there was no heat. Whoever was in the front room moved out, and we moved into the room with sun. Later, we got an apartment with a balcony. At some point during that year, there was a movie being made up in Bologna, and we all rushed off to work in the movie. Bill and Angelo were there doing the props. I think Bill White went up and got sick. We lived in Bologna for a month in the spring of 1950. The sun seemed to come up at 4 a.m. and came pouring in the windows. We'd be out walking around in the streets, and it would be like noon by the time it was 7 a.m. I spent a little time in southern France, in Vallauris, which was all ceramicists, making pots. Picasso was there at the time.

And then we came back to New York and moved into the 29th Street apartment, which we had either rented before going to Italy and sublet, or rented then. That was when apartments were still scarce and you had to get them through the grapevine. We all settled down to start a life of art. That was 1950 or '51. I guess none of us was fit for anything else.

Sally Hazelet Drummond with her son at the
Speed Art Museum, Louisville, mid-1960s

SALLY HAZELET DRUMMOND

November 21, 1974

In high school there was a little art there in the background, but nothing terribly major. I took art. I guess I kind of took art. I never felt I had any particular talent. Then I went to Rollins [College] in Florida, and I took art as an elective. I took sculpture from Constance Ortmayer. She kind of liked Maillol: serene, full, simple figures. She was a very nice teacher, though I wouldn't say I got much encouragement.

Then I went to Columbia for three years. I didn't know what I wanted to major in. The way I got to Columbia was funny. I knew somebody whose name was Marlon Brando, and his two sisters told me about a school called The New School. I had wanted to go to New York for years.

When I was nine, my father had won an award for an elevated highway, sponsored by U.S. Steel Corporation, and he decided we should all go up to New York — he, my mother, my sister, and I. I was never so thrilled by anything in my young life, and I never forgot it. We stayed in a hotel on Park Avenue, The Marguery, and it was wonderful. Before coming to New York to go to school, I had gone to a school in Washington, D.C., because my sister and husband were there, and my parents thought they would be company.

So, then came New York. My father came with me and we saw the dean of The New School. She was a gray-haired woman whose office and desk were covered with books and papers. My father took one look at the casual, somewhat slapdash atmosphere and said, "Let's go up to Columbia/Barnard." Up at Columbia, the dean asked where I had studied and what were my grades. I told her two years at Rollins. She said, "We consider a Rollins 'B' a 'C.'" And she suggested I apply across the street at the School of General Studies.

I didn't know what to take as a major. I thought of English, Philosophy, and Art. When you get down to academic restrictions, you have to make up your mind. So I decided on Art. And then, I didn't know whether I wanted it to be sculpture or painting. And then they said, "You have to decide." So I said, "Well, I'll be in the painting program." It was always swimming upstream. Because when I got to Columbia I felt not very good. I wasn't very facile. Making a figure like a figure? I couldn't do it — I didn't want to do it. I don't know which came first. It might have been a little of each.

I remember I had a teacher in a life drawing class. He wanted us to paint the model as it was. Well, I painted her in stockings and a garter belt, and I painted her green. I felt terribly German when I was doing it — I felt like Kurt Weill. I felt I had an idea, I was having fun. He came up about once every two weeks — he was sort of a gray eminence up there — and he said to me, "Why did you paint her green?" That was where everything fell away. He really just never looked at it the way you wanted him to look at it.

But I do remember painting one painting once. I had gone to see Gian Carlo Menotti's *The Medium* — it was the first time it was at the Heckscher Theater — and I came back and I painted a picture of . . . you know the story. There's a fat lady who had a crippled son and a wraith of a daughter. So I painted a picture of the wraithlike girl in a room with half walls, busted out windows. I just had a feeling I wanted to paint this picture all out of my head, so I did that. And I did about two or three others and I really felt fabulous about that. I lived on the East Side, on 115th Street, and I had to take a crosstown bus to school — this was in the springtime, and I really sailed across. I really felt good, I remember that.

My family was small. There were my mother and my father, Frances and Craig Hazelet, my sister, Sue, and that's it. My sister is two years and nine months older, and she lives in Kentucky now with her husband and three children. Mother and Father live there, but we were raised in Winnetka, a suburb of Chicago. And then we moved to Libertyville, Illinois — which was sort of in the country — when I was sixteen. I remember because it was just before Pearl Harbor, 1941. Mother wanted to get to the country. We had a cute little house in Winnetka. It was probably built in the '20s, an imitation saltbox, right across from the public high school, New Trier, the township high school. In 1941, mother had this idea of going out to the country, so we all went out to the country, and Daddy liked it. We all liked it. I finished high school at New Trier, but I can't remember how I got in to town. I must have come in with Daddy.

Daddy came from O'Neill, Nebraska. That was where he was born. His father was a superintendent of schools, and he also had a chicory farm. I'm not sure what they used it for — I know it goes into coffee. It was a tiny town. My grandfather had two sons, and he wanted to better himself, as he said. So he went to Alaska in the Gold Rush of 1898. He went off with two men and he kept a journal, which we just found recently, meticulously kept: what materials and equipment he required.

Here he was from the flatlands of Nebraska, with tumbleweed, and he forms a party and goes to Seattle. And they went up to Valdez, the Glacier Valdez, and up in the Copper River, and he kept this journal. My grandmother never thought she'd see her husband again. The letters were, of course, slow in coming. They'd have to go back to Valdez to get the mail and send it. They did find gold. They staked out a claim, they went back to O'Neill, Nebraska, and formed another party of twenty-six men and fourteen horses. He went back up to Alaska, and there were claim jumpers up there. And they were faced with this decision — whether they were going to shoot it out or go back to Juneau where the courts were, which was all the way back down the mountain, down the glacier. Well, he decided to go back down to Juneau. The upshot of the whole thing was Grandfather did not make a lot of money from gold. But he stayed in Alaska. He brought his wife and his two sons up there, and he built his house in Cordova. He was just thrilled by Alaska. He thought the real frontier and the future of America was up there. Loved the country, liked the people, and he kept this really marvelous journal, in which he describes the Gold Rush — his going up in the wilderness, man against nature, with droves of people going up at a time, all side by side. And how people were foolish, how they weren't well organized. They turned themselves into pack rats, gathering up their goods and going up the mountain and making camp and then resting and then going on. They had a boat — they had to build it. And when he went up with twenty men, they had to have horses and made their own wagons, made the wheels, and fording rivers, and how some were foolish and didn't look at it right and didn't figure it out right. But grandfather, he was a modest and a cautious and careful person. That was grandfather.

Grandmother was musical. She played the church organ in Cordova, and my father lived there nine years. My father lived there from the age of nine until he went to the University of Washington. His brother went there, too. My father majored in Civil Engineering. He went to M.I.T. for graduate work. He went there for a year and then World War One started. He was in the war. He never went overseas though. Then he worked for the Ford Motor Company in Detroit, and that's where he met my mother. She was born in Michigan, lived in Detroit. Then he left the Ford Motor Company, took a job as an instructor at the University of Illinois for three years. And my sister was born there, in Champaign, Illinois, in 1922. Then he got an opportunity to take over a company, the Scherzer Rolling and Lift Bridge Company in Chicago. I can't remember the exact details but they were very dramatic. The man either committed suicide or died very suddenly. Through a professor down in Illinois, my father was introduced to Mrs. Scherzer. Daddy said he had to go up there and read through the files and get a bead on the company. He was offered the job, and he took over this bridge design company.

Anyway, eventually it became Hazelet & Erdal. Erdal was an engineer from Norway and the technical man. So Daddy had this firm and still does, he's retired. They now have offices in Chicago, Cincinnati, Louisville, and Washington. The bridges they've built are all over. He has two in Louisville, a cantilevered bridge called the John F. Kennedy Bridge, and the Sherman Minton Bridge, which is a tied-arch bridge, a very pretty bridge, and was awarded the first prize for the most beautiful bridge designed in 1962 or '63 by the American Institute of Steel Construction. He has two bridges over the Mississippi at St. Louis and Memphis. In West Virginia he has one or two bridges, and he has bridges in Michigan. He designed seven bridges in France, two in Spain, and two in China. And they're mostly cantilevered bridges or tied-arch bridges. I don't think he's ever done a suspension bridge, but there aren't many of those. He's done elevated highways and a lot of expressway work. During the war, he designed a Static Test Laboratory in Dayton for the Army Air Force. It's a building in which they actually pick up these enormous planes and drop them. It's a test of the strength of their structure and the stresses and strains on them. And he's done some marine design for the Navy, mostly bridges and highways.

When my mother met my father, her name was Gillam. My mother's father took his own life, and then my grandmother remarried and they lived in Detroit. Mother was an only child. She taught piano, and they were married pretty soon after they met. Mother went to college for about one or two years at what was then called Kentucky College for Women and is now called Center College. We didn't have a lot of family because my paternal grandfather died when I was six years old. My grandmother died, I think, in childbirth, and my grandmother on Mother's side died soon after Mother and Daddy were married and her first husband was long gone. Her second husband she always referred to as Mr. Darrin, and Mother always called him Mr. Darrin, so there was no closeness. Anyway, there were no grandparents. Daddy had a brother, but he was living in Alaska, so although we celebrated all the American holidays, our family gatherings were small, mostly cousins from Chicago.

When we lived in Libertyville, we were about seventeen, ten miles from Chicago, about forty-five minutes on the train. Mother would always take us to Dr. Frederick Stock's Children's Concerts at the Chicago Symphony. I remember seeing a van Gogh show at the Art Institute. We used to go there quite often. I say quite often, maybe once a year. I did see real paintings. I must have been ten or twelve, fourteen maybe. And we used to go to the theater. I remember seeing

Philadelphia Story with Katherine Hepburn. We saw Helen Hayes in plays. *Victoria Regina* was one. We saw the opera. We saw *Carmen*, *Lucia di Lammermoor*.

I think the only time I've been consciously thrown by live art was Florence, seeing the live architecture of Florence. I can remember it palpably, physically feeling the elements, the proportions and the humanity of Florentine architectural forms, which I'd seen in magazines, but I'd never stood in it. I felt it more than paintings. I feel sometimes that people in one art are moved more by another art. I can be terribly moved by films, architecture, and sculpture. I love sculpture. I have a very hard time being sent by a painting. I'm a very poor tourist. Going around to museums, I get tired. I'd like to go around in a wheelchair. I do think, though, at all ages people are really looking. I remember some Vuillards that really exalted me much later. I think even with a lot of exposure you don't get jaded if you really love beauty.

Anyway, in our house, Mother liked music. Daddy liked music, and I played the piano a little, but I wouldn't say it was a heavy music scene. Also, in the house we had a little drawing of the house, and we had two Holbein prints, etchings. They were beautiful. That was about all. My sister Sue and I also had our portraits painted in oil by a professional portrait painter who was a friend of the family.

So after high school there was Rollins, Columbia, and then I went to the University of Louisville, Kentucky, for a master's degree. My family had moved there, Mother and Father. The paintings I was doing were figurative. They were like figures, all very slapdash and expressionistic. I'm trying to remember if I knew de Kooning's work then. This would have been 1952, and I hadn't been in New York since about 1949. I'm not sure I'd seen de Kooning's work — unless I had seen it in magazines. But there was lots of color, black lines. I did one called *The Magician*, everything very distorted, but figurative.

Then I applied for a Fulbright, and I got that, and I went to Venice. On the boat going over was [Charles] Cajori, who had a Fulbright and whom I'd known vaguely at Columbia. He was going to Rome, and I was going to Venice. He mentioned that he was with a little gallery called the Tanager Gallery and said that when I got back if I'd like to bring some work around, and if they liked it . . .

I bought one painting in Italy. I saw an Italian painter in the Biennale, a drawing by Alberto Burri. I traced him down to Rome and visited him. He's very nice. I liked his work and asked him how much were they, and he said, "They're very expensive." He said, "One hundred dollars." It was a hundred dollars. I paid that for a collage. Well, it wasn't a collage — it was burlap, and painted and sewn. It was about three feet square. That was 1953.

This was my first trip to Europe. I didn't want to go to the museums. I just wanted to sit in the cafes and see those wonderful . . . I was just floating for about the first six weeks, five weeks, however long it is you float. I just wanted to sit in the cafe and see the rhythm of the city, the people promenading every day. It was just fascinating — the food, the smells, first in Perugia and then Venice. I lived in Venice with two Americans from Louisville. We found an apartment and stayed there the year.

I hated Venice. I felt trapped. It was like living in a Jo Mielziner set. Everything was a stage set. It was beautiful. It was quiet, gentle. There was no violence. Nobody drank too much that you knew of. Very peaceful. Venice had no effect on my art at all. Europe, the whole thing of Europe, had no effect on my painting. It broadened me, it gave me a prospective on being an American. I didn't think that the experience strengthened my resolve.

I just felt grateful to my parents. They, so far, had supported me, with a little bit of doubt. By this time I was twenty-one or twenty-two, and I didn't have any credentials, except I'd gotten the Fulbright. Now that impresses. That's something like a notch in the belt. It helps. The Fulbright gives you a feeling of identity, and the program was terrific. It gave you a great deal of freedom. It was a marvelous thing of tact and respect.

But that thing in Florence, seeing the architecture, was a great moment. There was something about Renaissance Florence. I went to the Uffizi and saw the Leonardo *Annunciation*, which I remember loving, and the Botticelli. I don't see how anybody could not like that, just the grace.

My paintings were getting more and more non-objective, and I found it very difficult to live in Venice. We were living in a 1912, cold, high-ceilinged apartment in Venice. You'd go to bed with your mittens on, socks on, and didn't bathe all winter in the apartment. We went to the public baths. That was a tremendous experience, that and Florence. The public baths were terrific. The men would come to the baths with their briefcases and take out their underwear.

I read a lot of American novels. I read *The Scarlet Letter*, *Moby Dick*, Emily Dickinson. We'd go to USIS, the library, because they had the only place that had open-stock shelves. And they were also in English. I became the biggest American, but it wasn't conscious — it just happened. I guess the word is *homesick*. It was the only time in my life I ever felt homesick. I felt absolutely uprooted. And I found myself not a bit in touch with the Mediterranean personality. I felt so much like a square WASP. And I didn't want to offend anybody. I wouldn't wear slacks in 1952. I wanted to be a chameleon. I wanted absolutely to become anonymous and watch. But I couldn't because people would always say I was German, English, American. So I was there from September to July 4th. Then Cajori and I took a train to France. This was after a year of being homesick. I wasn't really homesick a year — maybe three months.

The couple I lived with [Jack and Allison] were American. They'd gotten married in Rome by a Polish priest from Chicago because Allison was pregnant. And they had the baby in the apartment in Venice. They had a midwife. They'd just been married, and they were having their thing, and it was all difficult. The whole period was difficult, cold and difficult. They were poor and difficult, and I had to give them some of my Fulbright money. They were going to be tossed out any time. The *questura* kept coming around, a Sicilian with a big red face yelling at us. So they got permission to stay until the baby was born, and they finally had to leave when the baby was six weeks old because Jack had no money. And the Italians were very touchy and nervous about poor Americans.

When they left, I moved into a *palazzo* — the top floor of a cold *palazzo*. But it was spring by then. Cajori and I took a train out of Venice. I've forgotten how we got together. We got off at Nice. I felt, "I've found my country." It's so weird. I just adored France. I think people just have their countries. It's chemistry. Venice in winter is damp, damp, damp, damp. I want to go back though. Everything is so subjective. Cajori had to go off to Paris, and I found a place west of Cannes. We went for a drink there, and I wanted to go back, so I did and stayed there for three weeks until I had to leave because the boat was leaving. It was heavenly, such a beautiful spot.

Then I decided I wanted to be in New York, and so I found an apartment on Charlton Street, the top floor of one of those houses. I paid very little rent, and I took care of the kids. The Klaws, Spencer and Bobbie Klaw.

I went around to the Tanager and showed them what I had. My paintings were all painted with lacquer, and they were very abstract. I'm getting simpler by this time. The thing about abstract expressionism that really kind of bothered me was I didn't feel that everything was necessary. De Kooning to me is abstract expressionism, and I find him so exciting and real. And he was the only one. He was the only one. Kline I liked but not like I liked de Kooning. And I was influenced by de Kooning, although he'd probably never see it.

But the thing of getting less from a sense of necessity — not being driven there, but rather of being drawn up to simplicity — I finally got down to an empty canvas. There were just a few dots, a few little shaggy forms covered with a network of color, lacquer on masonite, and then I'd begin to eliminate what I didn't think was necessary, and by gum, I got down to an empty canvas. I got to a square painting, and then I got to just a heaviness in the center. By this time I was painting with a four-inch sable brush and painting very thinly, thin lacquer. Very shiny. Paul Brach made a terrible statement once. He said, "I could comb my hair in Sally Hazelet's paintings." They were shiny and they were empty so he could see himself. And they were pretty. They weren't very much at all. But the Tanager took me on.

I found friends in New York compatible. I suppose I was lonely but content. And it was lively. There was a lot of life on Tenth Street — the openings, the people in the gallery, and there was a lot of interest in the Tanager. I looked at paintings. I respected Ad Reinhardt a lot, and I loved de Kooning — I just couldn't help being excited by de Kooning. I liked the austerity of Ad Reinhardt. I liked what seemed to me a kind of purity, maybe it was like a black mass he was performing, but I liked his austerity. Rothko I liked less. I felt he was less. He may have been more of a painter, but I liked the stringency in Reinhardt. I liked Guston's paintings very much. Guston's paintings, I guess, I liked the best in a very personal sense — the combination of simplicity and paint, that French Impressionist paint, those paintings in the '50s, pink and gray, centrally organized. I thought they were beautiful, and I still like them.

Mother and Daddy supported me before and during this time. At first, my painting habits were weak. I can remember there was always a little tension. My parents being middle class, Mother would always say, "You say you want to be a painter, why don't you paint?" This was when we were in Louisville. At the beginning of everything, it's always so hard. You don't know what you're going to do. And I didn't want to be influenced — I didn't want to mimic other people. Sometimes I feel I don't have a natural gift, whatever that is. It didn't come very easily, and I didn't want to be facile, as if there were any danger of that. I don't think there ever was. I didn't have the technical thing. I wanted to find my own "voice." I guess everybody has that same thing. You don't want to imitate and yet you are imitating. So you go out there and you try and think of a new idea, you know, so you don't do very much. Anyway, my work habits weren't very organized in the beginning. I guess by the time I got to New York and was living with the Klaws, I was painting.

But the biggest thing was the show at the Museum of Modern Art of Seurat. It was a huge show. They showed *A Sunday on La Grande Jatte* from the Art Institute of Chicago, which I had grown up with. I just loved that show, and I loved the energy of all those points. I was painting those flat lacquer paintings, which were pretty dull, nothing. In other words, I think I had an idea, and I didn't know how to fill it out, flesh it out. I still don't, but I'm closer. But Seurat, with those dots, he has three paintings . . . they're studies for *The Bathers*, they're about this big, and they belong to the Louvre, and there's one of a back, and there's one of a profile nude, and one is standing. They're eventually incorporated in the one painting. The back, this one painting of the back, it's so plain, and it's so beautiful, just the form, the color. It has a huge scale, and it's a little painting. It's a lovely painting. I love his lithographs, the blackness, the energy in them. Sometimes Seurat's sort of precious, but I love those little points of color. So I went back and started putting blobs of paint to try to activate this idea, fill it out, and that really had a big impact.

At the time I had no notion of supporting myself by painting. I'm not a great one to think about the future in big terms, not that big. It was the GALLERY UPTOWN, in capital letters — that was our big ambition as I remember it. And a review in the *Times*. Those were the concerns. In one early show, Dore Ashton said something to the effect, "There's not a great deal to see in Sally Hazelet's paintings, so I guess there really isn't very much to say." And that's about right, too. That was about 1954.

Al Held in his New York studio, c. 1956

AL HELD

December 1, 1974

In my mother and father's house there was this portfolio of van Gogh reproductions that they got from *The New York Post* for a buck. They're hanging in their house now, to this day, and still framed in these goofy frames. I never took it as art. I remember it was on a spiral wire, a pad kind of thing, and you had to rip each one off and cut it to frame it. But I never thought of it as art. The first real art I got in contact with was much later, after I came out of the Navy. It was actually hanging around a political social club here in Manhattan. Nick Krushenick was part of this club. He had just gotten out of the Army, and I had just gotten out of the Navy, and we'd hang around there. It was a cultural club, a folk cultural club, called "Folksay."

Nick wanted to be an artist and started going to the Art Students League. We lived in the same part of the Bronx, and we'd go down to this club once or twice a week and come back on the subway together. We got to be friendly, and I kept tripping out on his fantasies about the great paintings he was going to paint. That must have been 1948, '49, somewhere around then. That was the first art, probably, outside of the van Gogh prints. The club had only to do with folk music and dancing, and Nick's brother used to be a folk dance caller, the whole bullshit. Nick was the only person I had ever met who had aspirations.

I was born in Brooklyn. I know my family had lived in another part of Brooklyn, but my memory goes only as far back as Brownsville. By the time of Brownsville, I must have been five or six; I have a younger sister, who was born by that time. I went from Brownsville to Bedford-Stuyvesant in the middle of the Depression. My father was a jeweler and worked in a factory. Of course, it was a factory with a luxury product, and they were the first to lose their jobs.

My memories of early childhood are of the Depression, welfare, and the rest of that shit. In the middle of the Depression, my family had this opportunity to buy a pickle and herring stand — not a store, a stand, outside, you know, the barrels of pickles and herring outside — in Bedford-Stuyvesant on DeKalb Avenue. I remember this very clearly. It cost three hundred bucks, and my father barely raised it by begging, borrowing, and stealing every penny he could get from everybody he knew — relatives. We lived in an apartment above the stand until the beginning of World War Two. The Depression didn't end until the war began. My father gave up the stand then and went back into the jewelry business.

We all worked in the stand. That was a change in my life. I worked there whenever he could catch me. It was rough. It was from about 6 a.m. in the morning until 9 p.m. at night. The stench never left us. It was up in the apartment, the bedrooms, everyplace. That's when I started getting very rambunctious and rebellious. I started playing hooky from school and going off by myself and stealing, or just running around.

It was those years. They were rough years for my parents — and obviously, rough years for me. I used to run with a steady group, but then I'd go off by myself. I'd go to Times Square. I must have been thirteen. I knew how to sneak into every movie house on Times Square. There was a different system for each one. The penalty for getting caught was not being put in jail — it was getting the shit kicked out of you by the ushers. But I did that alone. I used to like to go up there and sit in those dark holes and then go out to Grant's for lunch and back into the dark hole for the afternoon. I sneaked in the side doors, the fire exits. There were some places you couldn't get in any way except through the front. I used to wait until the feature was over and everybody would pile out, and you'd needle your way through. The big-time movie houses I used to sneak into, but the little movie houses on 42nd Street, there was no sneaking into because it wasn't classy enough to sneak into. That I'd pay for. The bands were playing then, and I would go to the bands and what have you, but I wasn't much interested in the bands — it was the films. The darkness and the films more than the bands. All the movies impressed me. Any films from the 1940s, I know backwards and forwards. There isn't a movie I didn't see.

When my father went into the jewelry business again, we moved to the lap of luxury, the East Bronx. It was Crotona Park North. It was pretty around there. The East Bronx was put down as compared with West Bronx, but for us — coming up from Brooklyn, from Bedford-Stuyvesant — it was spectacular. Right across the street was a park, a playground, and a swimming pool. It was like going to the suburbs.

When I moved up there, I must have been about fifteen and a half, because I only spent about a year and a half in high school. I went to about six high schools. I think the last high school I went to was Roosevelt High. Then I got to be sixteen. On my sixteenth birthday, my mother was called into school by the assistant principal, or the dean of boys, who said — I'll never forget this — "Mother," — and he did use the word "Mother" — "it would be better for the child, better for you, better for the school, if your child left school. Good-bye." I wasn't a wise-ass kid. It was more like passive resistance, non-co-operation. I'd just go off someplace, do whatever I wanted to do. I wouldn't take on a teacher or get into a fistfight with a teacher, like other kids did. I'd just cut out. I had no trouble with kids, but I could take it or leave it. I had some friends, but they were from the street, and they may have gone to that school or not gone to that school. It wasn't very significant.

My sister had gotten a good, healthy case of asthma years before, and my mother had taken her to Arizona for a year, in desperation. Then she was shipped off to a home in Denver, and by the time I had gone to the Bronx, when I was sixteen, she was either just coming back from Denver or was still out there, so I didn't see very much of her in those years.

I went to work at different kinds of jobs. Anything from my father trying to make me into a jeweler, which didn't last more than two or three days, or shipping clerks. All kinds of stuff, all the shlock kid jobs. I was too neurotic to dislike anything. It was more like: "It's nice down there on the street there. I'd like to go down there." And I'd get up and go. I didn't think anything through. It was much more emotional. "I'd rather be there, so I'll go there. Fuck it." I didn't even say, "Fuck it."

I wasn't passive about my feelings towards my father though. I hated my father. My father used to beat on me, and I used to try to ridicule him any way I could.

My parents met in America, but they were born in Russia and Poland. My father came here when he was in his early twenties. He was a student, he was a soldier in the Austro-Hungarian Army in World War One, and then he went to Budapest and learned the jewelry trade. My father tells it — and he's not very communicative — that his father had some relatives here that were doing all right, and his father decided he should go to America. He was the oldest.

My mother came here when she was four. The whole family came, and whatever is left of them is still here. She went to school here — only grade school — and then she left. She lived on the Lower East Side. In fact, when I came back from the Navy and moved out of the house, I took a cold-water flat on the Lower East Side. It nearly broke my mother's heart: "Thirty years, thirty years, struggling to get away from that place, and you move two blocks away."

At that age, sixteen, when we moved to the Bronx, I never had any real girlfriends — more like, I'd go out with girls and try to have sex with them, and sometimes I did, and sometimes I didn't. But no real steady dating with anybody, no attachment.

At sixteen I went into the Navy, to Camp Perry, Virginia. I thought I would have a nice time. I was very anxious to get in, but for a Jewish father to sign a boy into the Navy at sixteen was radical. It really made his life miserable. I didn't much like it once I got in. I must have been a real malcontent, a neurotic kid. I didn't much like it. All the fights I got into in the Navy were with Southerners who had a different kind of mentality. I'd just call somebody a son of a bitch, and they'd say, "You're calling my mother a bitch?" And they'd try to kill me. And you'd sort of stand around and say, "What's happening?" "Where am I?" I didn't much care for the officers. It was passive resistance, more like just copping out.

I got put on a submarine tender. I went down to Panama, moved around Panama and the Caribbean. I only signed up for two years, and I got out. I liked the traveling, that was nice — I enjoyed that. They wanted me to sign up again. They offered me everything. I knew I didn't want to do that. I was heading for California and was just stopping back to see my mother and father. She had some money that I had sent to save for me. But she wouldn't give it to me, so I didn't go to California.

The only book I read in two years in the Navy was on night watch down in Panama. I went to the ship's library and took this book out, and looking back on it now it was a kind of funny book to read: *The Fountainhead*. I had no contact with art and literature before. It simply didn't exist. It wasn't that I was hostile towards it; it simply wasn't part of my consciousness. I had nothing to do with it. It wasn't that I didn't want to go to a museum. It didn't exist. So it was interesting that I read *The Fountainhead*.

When I came home, I hung around the Bronx. I was on the "52-20" on the G.I. Bill — unemployment that they gave to servicemen. I was just hanging around doing nothing. Just really hanging out. Then a couple of guys asked me if I wanted to go to Greenwich Village and help build some May Day floats. My father had been a leftist. I had been in so many May Day parades that I wasn't horrified by the suggestion. But what interested me was Greenwich Village with all those free women. We actually ended up in Pete Seeger's house, and we walked into the house, and there was a baby, sitting bare-assed on the floor, shitting on the floor. I was very shocked by it. I hung around there a couple of days helping build these floats and made a couple of passes at girls that put me down very hard with the implication, as I remember, that I was an uncouth schmuck from the Bronx, which I took great offense in and felt really put down.

This was the core group of this cultural left-wing group called Folksay. They're the ones who started all the square dancing in the city and started singing those funky folk songs in Washington Square Park. Dreary, terrible, awful. The Weavers came out of that group. This was a left-wing group, but my intellectual life was nil. My father was political, and the house was full of radical politics. Not radical —

Marxist, the most orthodox. My father was of the orthodox left wing. What I'm saying is that I wasn't typically American, in the sense that I wasn't horrified by the mention of Marxism or Communism. This was part of this whole upbringing — part of the household — so that I didn't have to go through an intellectual exercise to accept it or reject it. It was just a normal thing. So I became socially connected with these people and joined this club. We worked very hard for the Henry Wallace campaign. We organized agitprop theater. We went on the backs of trucks all through that campaign, through Harlem doing skits.

I met the Krushenicks, who were living in the Bronx. Nick was, but John lived downtown. We used to go home together. In the Bronx, part of the culture was that every elevated stop had a candy store, a liquor store, a drug store, and a cafeteria, like a little village nestled around it, open all night. We used to get off at his stop or my stop and go to the cafeteria, and we began to buddy up. At that time, I had decided I was going to go back to school and get my high school diploma and go on to college and become a social worker and become socially productive. But I got more and more interested in Nick's business, and I thought I'd like to try this art business, too, on the G.I. Bill. All my friends began to laugh and do double spins: "What? You?" I got very ashamed and very uptight about it and decided I wasn't going to use the G.I. Bill for it. I would go and take a couple of drawing courses on my own to see if I liked it, at the Art Students League. I liked it, and I decided in the fall I would invoke the G.I. Bill and go there.

By that time, I had become very political and had moved downtown. I began painting seriously as a student. And I was very socially conscious with the G.I. Bill: social realist paintings, Negroes hanging from trees — I was painting that type of painting. Then at that time, 1948 to '49, Joe McCarthy and the whole thing about the Rosenbergs was happening, and the Rosenbergs lived just about a block away from me. So there was really a lot of uptight feeling, like fascism had arrived. I decided I was going to get out of the country and pack it in. I decided I was going to Mexico to study with Siqueiros, the real painter of social realism. I had it all set up and then there was some shoot-out scandal in Mexico. Siqueiros got shot at or shot somebody else, and they closed the school down. I couldn't go there, but by that time I had psyched myself up to get out.

I had been working at the Art Students League night and day. Working in two classes, painting and drawing, and another eight hours as a dishwasher to get enough money to get out. I had opened up the school and closed it up for about six or eight months by that time. So, it didn't make any difference where I went. I just wanted to go. So, I said, "What about Paris? I'd go to Paris instead." Which I did.

I stayed there three years.

All the social obligations got lifted. For about two months in Paris I swore I would never see another American again. I hung out with French leftists. Got fed up with them and began hanging out with Americans. Yeah, a terrific sense of freedom, because I had no intellectual or moral obligations. More importantly, though, was no intellectual obligations. Emotional obligations were tough enough, but the intellectual obligations were surprisingly heavy, too. It's very hard to make changes when you've got these intellectual alliances. You feel you're betraying a friend by making one move or another. I didn't have to explain myself to anybody, friend or foe. It was fantastic.

I also became very pro-American and began to look at American paintings there. I had seen Pollock before I left, and I couldn't quite adjust it to my social-realist prejudices. I finally rationalized it. Pollock was okay because he was really a social realist, he was painting violence and speed. I began to get influenced by American painting in Paris. But, again, I didn't have the intellectual loyalties and obligations I had in New York.

You have to remember, when I finally got to Paris I had been in art one year, maybe two, so I was still very much a dumb student. But, in hindsight, one interesting thing was that, as dumb as I was, my kindergarten education in art was in the Museum of Modern Art. And when I went to Paris, I went from gallery to gallery and from museum to museum. I went to the modern art museum, saying, "But I'm not seeing the real thing. Where is the real stuff?" I was trained just by osmosis, by going into the Museum of Modern Art and seeing those paintings there. I didn't know if they were good paintings or bad paintings, but those were paintings, and they became the average experience. That's what painting was. There were those Matisses, those Picassos, Cézannes, those this and those that. I didn't claim to understand them or see deeply into them, but my eyeball got accustomed to seeing those paintings.

When I went to Paris, I didn't see that stuff. But after a while, I discovered that there wasn't anything in Paris, and I wasn't making a mistake. The modern museum in Paris now has got a lot of work, but in 1950 it was empty. So it turned out, as I am fond of saying, that a French painter of my age, at that time, hadn't seen good French painting as I had. That seemed crazy. It wasn't an intellectual analysis — it was the paintings that were around.

The Louvre was really stupendous, exciting. I remember spending a lot of time in the two grand halls with the Delacroixs and all the academic painters. I remember looking at *The Raft of the Medusa* trying to figure out, "What went wrong?" You know, they were such good paintings, what did they miss and how come? You look at those paintings, and those guys knew what they were doing. I remember

48

Continued on page 65

Ronald Bladen, *Connie's Painting*, c. 1956-59, oil on canvas, 38 x 35 1/2 inches.

Lois Dodd, *Pasture*, 1955, oil on linen, 39 x 60 inches.

Lois Dodd, *Cows in Landscape*, 1958, oil on linen, 44 x 51 inches.

Sally Hazelet Drummond, *Untitled*, 1959, oil on canvas, 18 x 18 inches.

Sally Hazelet Drummond, *Presence of the Heart*, 1962, oil on canvas, 60 x 60 inches.

Al Held, *Untitled,* 1954, oil on canvas, 26 x 32 inches.

Al Held, *Untitled,* 1955, oil on canvas, 71 x 83 inches.

Alex Katz, *Two Boys,* 1951, oil on board, 18 5/8 x 14 1/2 inches.

Alex Katz, *28th Street Loft*, 1954, oil on board, 48 1/4 x 32 inches.

William King, *Sally Hazelet*, 1952, glazed terra cotta, 10 3/4 x 5 1/2 inches.

William King, *Sick Man,* 1957, wood, 21 1/8 x 10 7/8 x 4 inches.

Philip Pearlstein, *The Capture*, 1954, oil on canvas, 48 x 40 inches.

Philip Pearlstein, *Tree Roots*, 1957, oil on canvas, 50 x 40 inches.

George Sugarman, *Four Forms in Walnut*, 1959, wood, 19 1/2 x 86 x 20 inches.

George Sugarman, *Yellow Top*, 1959, acrylic on wood, 89 x 46 x 34 inches.

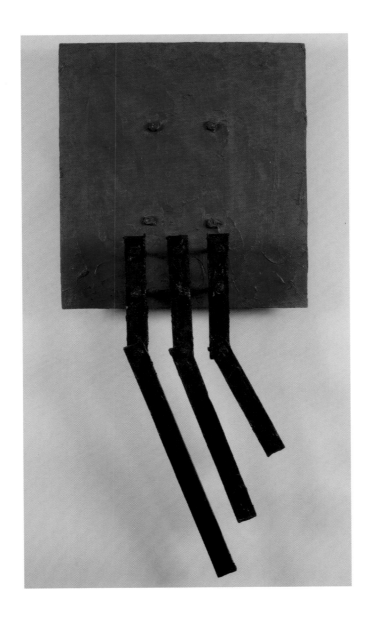

Ronald Bladen, *Green and Black*, 1961-62, wood painted with metal,
45 x 20 1/2 x 7 inches.

spending a lot more time trying to find out what was wrong with those paintings than what was right with other paintings. And I did a lot of painting in Paris. I started off with figures and ended up with four huge *Guernica*-esque figures. And I said, "Aha, I finally can paint or draw figures." It was a moralistic thing about the figure: wanting to paint abstractly for maybe six months — which was a long time in my experience — but saying, "No, I have to learn how to draw the figure first." Then doing something, which if I saw it today probably looks terrible, but was good enough for me to rationalize and say, "Ah, okay."

So then I started painting abstractly. I remember having this beautiful naive notion — to show you how naive I was — which came to me in a movie house. A light bulb lit up in my mind and I went, "Ha, if Mondrian is the apex of objectivity, and Pollock is the apex of subjectivity, it stands to reason if you put the two together, you will get a universal." So, I then went back to the studio and did precisely that. I would then divide up my canvas geometrically and within each geometric division would pour paint. Unfortunately. I even had a show with those things in Gallerie Huit.

Gallerie Huit was a co-op gallery in Paris run by Americans. That gallery started in 1951 and may have predated the New York co-ops on Tenth Street. [The Tanager Gallery opened on 4th Street in 1952 and on 10th Street in 1953. It was the first of the co-ops in New York.] You had to sit at your own show. So, I had the show for three weeks in 1952, and I even got some pretty nice put-down reviews from the French. The French treated the gallery with great serious hostility.

So, after doing these paintings, which I was really high on — unfortunately they've all been destroyed, except for one small one, which I still have, all the rest were either painted over or I threw away — at any rate, after sitting in the gallery for three weeks, I couldn't paint another one of those paintings. I think every artist should sit with his show for three weeks; I think styles would change radically.

Then I decided I wanted to do organic shapes. I can't remember how it started. I decided I didn't know how to draw, and I wanted to teach myself how to draw. So I started drawing from rocks. The rocks were abstract, and they had an organic shape and human feeling to them. I did hundreds of drawings from rocks. I used to go around Paris, picking up rocks and sitting them on a table and drawing from them.

I met George Sugarman in Paris. I met Sam Francis and Shirley Jaffe, too. Oh Jesus, I just blocked out all the names, there were so many people. Gabe Kohn. We all came back to the United States except Sam. There were two reasons. One was the G.I. Bill ran out.

It was dependent upon the length of service. Mine was three years. George had been in the Navy a much longer time, but the G. I. Bill, I think, had a limit of four years.

By that time, I had many, many more contacts in Paris than in New York. I had none in New York. I had left as a student, and I was becoming a young professional. I had this studio, and I had a choice to make. I had to choose to stay in Paris or to go back. I looked around me, and I saw Sam Francis was really beginning to make it. Other people weren't, but they were always hustling paintings. I decided that I didn't want to hustle paintings. I could have, I knew enough people, enough critics, enough this, enough that. But I decided I'd rather go back to New York and get a part-time job and paint, because I figured I'd spend more time hustling than I would at a part-time job.

With the G.I. Bill, you had to sign up in a school. You had to be affiliated. So I was actually signed up in a place called the Academy of the Grande Chaumière. Sam and a lot of other people were signed up with Léger. I went there to hear him give a crit once. I hated him. I hated his work. I thought it was just absolutely awful. It took years to actually appreciate it. When Léger was giving this crit, he hated being there teaching. I think he felt humiliated, because it was something he had to do, and he just sat there and mumbled.

I left Paris looking forward to getting back. I came back with two crates of paintings, schlepped to the Bronx. On the boat coming back, I said, "I bet that loft is still empty that I had looked at before I left, on East Broadway." Sure enough, I went back there, and the loft was sitting there empty. It was twenty dollars a month, and I moved into it and started fixing it up. Then I met a girl and got married very quickly, before I even knew her a week. It was an absolute disaster. To make a long story short, I ended up burning down that loft accidentally and lost a lot of paintings. Got wiped out.

Then I moved to a different apartment, with a different girl. Then I broke up with this girl. By that time, she had had a child, my daughter. I went over to Hoboken and spent six or eight months in Hoboken. I spent a year or so out on the West Coast and came back, because I couldn't find a job there.

When I first started going into art with Nick Krushenick, his father was a carpenter, and Nick and I both decided, because there was no money in art, we both were going to become carpenters. Work six months of the year to get enough money to live and paint for the other six months. And we both became apprentice carpenters in the union through Nick's father. When I went to Paris, I tore up that union card: "Boy, I don't like that at all, that's hard work!" When I went to San Francisco, I couldn't get a job anyplace. Industry was really tight, and the only place I could get a job was a construction job as a carpenter on these highways. I did, and I got myself an apartment and a studio and started to paint.

I met Yvonne Rainer out there, and we started living together. She had this pretty little one-story house in the middle of Broadway, up on a big hill in San Francisco. On either side of the house there were two houses that went up another story. I decided I was going to paint up on the roof. I had these two sidewalls to paint on. It was terrific, ideal. I brought this big canvas up there and I started painting away. I was using pigment, mixing my own colors, and I worked up there for about a month. I couldn't get anything going, and I took the painting down to the cellar of the house and finished it there. Just like a nice, dark, New York loft.

Then I came back to New York. In the middle 1950s, people like Pollock and de Kooning were beginning to make money, and those were people who were part of my world, our world. There were other artists who always made a lot of money, but they weren't part of my world, and it didn't mean anything. Picasso, Matisse, or Andrew Wyeth; good artists, bad artists. If they made a lot of money, that was like a movie star — someplace else and somebody else. So, it seems to me, and maybe this is hindsight, there was a slight shift there, like the blink of an eye.

Nobody really thought of selling paintings because nobody really did, except the older guys, but I think that was a beginning of hope. Four years before, on Tenth Street, it didn't happen. It didn't exist. This was the middle 1950s, when I came to Tenth Street. I hadn't sold any paintings, and I never thought about selling. Now there was a glimmer of hope.

Alex Katz in New York, 1956

ALEX KATZ

March 17, 1974

I was born at home in Sheepshead Bay, Brooklyn, on July 24, 1927. We lived on Crystal Street until I was one and a half years old. My mother's relatives moved in, my family moved to Queens. My parents, brother, and I lived at 115-46 173rd Street in St. Albans, where I spent all of my early years.

The St. Albans house was a two-story house with seven rooms, counting a closed front porch. There was an open back porch. The back yard had a garage with red rambling roses all over it and a peach tree (four peaches, which were very large the first year). The front yard was a small lawn, which my father could mow and trim in twenty minutes (with a hand mower and scissors), with a maple tree, which tipped over and pulled up part of the sidewalk, and a pine tree.

We always had dogs, several at a time. Some slept inside, some outside, some were only allowed in the hall. We had a chow called Chubby and a German shepherd called Jocko, who was taken through distemper twice by my parents. I walked Jocko, mostly. The others were really my father's dogs. He had a way with animals. He put a lot of attention into raising them and they were devoted to him. Chubby could recognize his car coming home. He'd get very excited. I never saw him hit a dog, but they always did everything he said.

I spoke Russian and Yiddish until I was four, when all foreign languages were cut off. My mother had me memorizing Jack London before I was four. Then my parents decided they didn't want a precocious child and turned my attention to other children in the neighborhood.

One day, I was standing on the top of the stairs, and my mother said she was going to the hospital and was going to bring home "something nice." I went to the hospital with my father, which was a wooden building with a porch, more like a house, not a regular hospital, and babies were crying, and I saw my mother. I guess I first saw my brother then. I don't remember their telling me his name. I later called him by name, Bernard. I didn't like having someone else around. He had a nice smile, I remember that. I can't remember whether I liked him as a baby, but I turned the carriage over, by accident, and he didn't get hurt. It was a big incident, a fuss was made over that. Very early, it was established that I could do just about everything I wanted, but I couldn't hit him.

My father didn't seem to do the things with my brother that he had done with me, probably because I was around to play with Bernard. Playing with Bernard was always a lot of fun. He was good natured, with a very nice sense of humor. When he was old enough to go out to play, everyone called him Bernie, and I started to call him Bernie. Although we went to the same elementary school, I never saw him there.

I once gave him trick chewing gum, which snapped back and hurt his fingers. I really felt bad. He was four. I was eight. And, he couldn't find the funnies in the newspapers fast enough. We raced for the funnies, and I always got them. He never knew where they were.

But Bernie was very tough. No one could make him do what he didn't want to do. You could break his arm, but he never walked away from fights. At some age in grammar school, he picked fights with boys for about six months, every day, until an older boy about his size beat him up. He was not a belligerent boy, but he enjoyed a fight.

Once, all the boys on the block wanted to see who could hang from a tree the longest. We could all climb to the branch we were going to hang from. Bernie was ten, and the oldest boy was seventeen. We picked a big, tall tree, and only two of us could climb it to the top — Bernie and Rodney Campbell, who was sixteen or seventeen. Bernie held on the longest, but climbing to the top of the tree was out of the question for me.

I went to kindergarten at four and quit halfway through. I didn't like it. I distinctly remember thinking that going to school meant the end of freedom. Mother was glad; she liked having me home.

Sima was what the family called my mother. Her stage name was Ella Marion in this country and maybe in the other countries too. She took piano lessons, speech lessons, read a lot, and she said she would have been a great star if she could sing and dance. I remember her bedroom, that's a distinct memory. Her bed was a bright yellow-green and had a velvet bedspread that was a soft dusty yellow, more towards beige. There was a dresser that was green, too. The wall color was also a soft color, a very light, dull shade of violet. This was my father's bedroom, too. He painted flowers on the velvet bedspread. They had an etching by a Jewish artist on the wall on the left. The artist's name was something like Tobat. It was of three nude people and was very weird. They were very long people with very small genitals. They had paintings hanging too. Some were oils of my mother when she was a student in Russia, one of her by the sea.

My crib was in another room. They told me the crib was an antique. They painted it orange and green, one stripe orange and one stripe green, a dark green, not a bright green. They both painted rooms and furniture, but my father was more involved in decorating. He put a pattern on the wall of the sun porch. The wall was a dusty salmon. The design was a dark bright red, sort of a triangular design with broken edges. It was painted very neatly. I don't think he used masking tape. I don't know how he did it. He painted plant holders orange and green, but they were painted very casually with drips coming down. They always bothered me because they were so sloppy.

My mother looked very different than she looks now. She had lots of red hair. She had a fuller mouth than in her middle years. I remember her teeth weren't so good. She had false teeth put in when I was a teenager, and that changed her face quite a bit. But the outstanding characteristic of her face is the wildness of the greenish-gray eyes. She still has them, even with glasses on.

At five, I went back to public school. After some years, it seemed that school was freedom, because people seemed to have to work the rest of their lives. I went to P.S. 140 in Jamaica, Queens, one quarter of a mile away from home, from the first through the eighth grade, skipping the last half of the seventh grade. When I was five years old, on weekends, my father took me out in the woods or on the porch, and we did watercolors together. My father's hands had more manual dexterity. I remember mine were childish, and my father's were more adult, but similar.

I remember him showing me buildings. There were new buildings in Addersley, part of St. Albans. They were private houses made of brick with slate roofs. We were looking at the construction, I guess. Addersley was a section about four or five blocks from where we lived, where all the blacks who made it lived: J.P. Johnson, Fats Waller, Jackie Robinson, Roy Campanella, Lena Horne. Fats Waller's kids went to the same public school I went to. And, I used to see J.P. Johnson going home from work a lot. He played piano in a white bar.

My father was very muscular. He looked like Tarzan. He bragged about how he cut the lawn. He had theories about mowing lawns. He never wanted to retrace his steps, so he mowed in concentric circles. He was quick. He worked furiously when he worked and left things all over the place. He must have left four hundred cans of used hall paint with rotting brushes in the cellar.

My father had a very strong will. I think that's why he and my mother moved to Queens, a community they had nothing in common with, which was very near the country — dirt roads, large truck farms — and why they spoke only English with me at an early age. He felt I was American and should be assimilated and be what I was, American.

My father didn't dress up much when he was older, but he was a sharp dresser as a young man. He had a way of wearing casual clothes that I couldn't appreciate until I was much older. He liked to wear suede jackets. I did get into his shirts and ties when I got to be his size. He had very good taste in shirts and ties; they could be worn always.

He was born in Lida, a small town in Russia. He studied to be a rabbi, but it didn't take. He said his blood was too hot. He had a large family. My father had a bunch of sisters who never came to America, and he had a brother who died when he was young, in a fire. His family owned a tile factory; they made porcelain stoves with ceramic tiles. His grandfather was a scholar but was poor and wanted to make money so he could study. He imported a German technician and started the stove business with what he had. My father's father was a scholar, too.

My father played billiards or pool a lot of the time in Europe for sport, and he ran his business, the tile business, from there. He rode horses over bridges and raced motorcycles across fields. He said he used to jump off bridges on horses.

My father came to the United States after the revolution, after spending several years in Berlin. My mother came to America a couple of years before he did, but they had known each other in Russia. They met in his hometown. She was an actress traveling through, and he was part of an amateur acting group. They needed a professional, he said.

During World War Two, what was left of my father's family disappeared in the part of Russia he was born in. His five or six sisters had all stayed there after the revolution. One day when I was a teenager, all of a sudden, he started to sing Peer Gynt. He had a bass voice and a very good one. It came as a big surprise. He was killed in a car accident when I was sixteen.

In the first grade, I was in the last seat in the last row. I didn't like the teacher, and I stayed out of school a lot that term. My mother thought it was okay. I won the Wanamaker Art Prize that term for a crayon drawing, colored in, of a tree with a lot of monkeys in it.

In the first half of the second grade, I was put into a slower class, because of my absences in the first grade. I got along better with the teacher. As the years went by, I did very well in English and Math, but I was bored much of the time and talked a lot. I read a lot too, after school and during summers. The public library was two blocks away from the house, and I used it. In the seventh grade, I got the second highest on the aptitude test (putting me at high school reading level) and was skipped to the eighth grade. Mr. Murphy, the principal, gave those of us who skipped class grammar lessons and told us, if we really got stuck, to use "who." That summer, at thirteen, I traded a pair of roller skates for two bushels of books. I read a novel every morning and played baseball every afternoon. I stayed in bed reading until noon. My mother thought that was okay. My friends came to get me for baseball after lunch. And I'd go to the beach with the family in the car when my father came home from work, and we'd swim and eat supper there.

When I was leaving P.S. 140, Mr. Murphy thought it a mistake to go to a trade school rather than an industrial arts school or [the High School of] Music and Art, but I chose Woodrow Wilson High School because they had more art classes than the academic high schools nearby. My parents suggested a local academic school and opposed Music and Art because of the distance.

Woodrow Wilson, originally the Jamaica Vocational High School, was an old wooden building. The majority of the kids were waiting until they were sixteen and could leave school. The first year, classes were full. But by the second year, the school was underpopulated. Less than one quarter of those who entered with me graduated. Most of the pupils had working papers by fourteen, including me. It was a co-ed school, predominantly boys though. When a new building was built, it became Woodrow Wilson Vocational High School. That was when I was still a freshman, and we moved there.

In high school, I played the violin in the orchestra, I was on the track team, and I did a lot of watercolors and drawings. I remember, as a freshman, spending fifteen minutes trying to determine where a line should be. It seemed there should be an exact place where the line should be and an exact angle. The teacher of the drawing class at Wilson had studied at the National Academy, but the class could do anything in the way of drawing. I drew from casts every day from lunch to 3:30 p.m., because I wanted to. I did this for a year and a half. I got good by then. I continued to draw from casts for three more years, though not on a daily basis. Cast drawing has a system, similar to systems in cubist art, controlling or breaking light harmonies and violating dark harmonies and knowing when one is doing it. Later, at Cooper Union when we did abstract cubist drawing, it was all logical and simple for me.

With watercolors, I had no system. They seemed like day labor. I felt very bad about all the work involved, very ineffective. Hard labor was not necessarily rewarding. I was amazed at how ugly hard labor got.

A friend, Ken Pfeiffer, an industrial designer, already out of high school, took me to see a Mondrian show at the Museum of Modern Art. It opened up a lot for me. Pfeiffer was two years older and studying at Pratt. He gave me books on Mondrian. I liked the paintings, but I didn't like what Mondrian wrote. I couldn't relate it to any experience. I was very art uneducated.

Another friend had a Cézanne book and lent it to me when I was in high school. I was very interested. I wanted to become a commercial artist. I had no idea that I could be a fine artist. I thought one had to be a genius.

During high school one summer, I worked doing paste-ups in an ad agency in New York, and did that for a while after graduating high school and before entering the Navy. I met Jimmy Stevenson at work. He was very important in my life. He had a skeptical mind. He gave me as much in this area as Ken Pfeiffer had in introducing me to art.

The students at Woodrow Wilson were completely divorced from culture, but they really knew a lot about popular culture. One of the teachers, Mr. De Santa, thought the kids' music was crap, but he allowed us to bring in records, and there were many discussions about jazz and jazz musicians and groups and arguments about why Ziggy Elman was good or had an intellectual nature.

The only art form I knew at that time was dancing. We all danced. Woodrow Wilson had great dancers, and there was a jukebox in the lunchroom. The whole area around the school was focused on dancing. There were always discussions on style or the possibilities of a style of dancing. The basic local style was the "Jamaica Drape," which was a half-time Lindy and moved on the half beat or even on the quarter beat if the music was very fast. It was a restrained, reductive type of dance, and one was supposed to be able to dance it to a waltz, tango, or anything. The fast, hop-type Lindy was frowned upon, as it was felt to restrict a person's style in the dance.

I had different jobs while I was going to high school in the early 1940s. One was night watchman on the railroad that crossed Jamaica Bay. If there was a fire, the watchman had to put it out. If a train came, there were tie extensions he could stand on. If he wasn't near one, he had to jump into the bay or get hit by a train. A great job. I'd go straight to the beach after work every morning. While I was making money working, part-time or summers, I bought clothes. I bought great zoot suits at Nemser Brothers on Broadway and Waverly, a great zoot suit house. They were made to order for about twenty dollars (a week's pay). By the time I graduated from high school, I had seven zoot suits.

After high school, I wanted to be a gunner in the Navy Air Force. I passed the test but not with a high enough grade. I remember missing a question about turning a corner and traction. And I remember meeting a guy there from Brooklyn who told me, "What a great race you ran for Woodrow Wilson." I felt bad about missing gunner and had always liked heights, so rather than being drafted, I joined the regular Navy.

I went to boot camp in Geneva, N.Y., on V.J. Day. I had joined the Navy for the duration plus six months. I had a great time in the Navy, I felt free. The war was over. I left on a ship called *The Hermit-*

age, a seized Italian luxury-liner troop ship. The first port we hit was Marseilles. They gave us a lecture: "100,000 prostitutes and lots of V.D." And they handed the sailors "pro" kits as they went down the gangplank.

I was up for a scholarship to Pratt before I went into the Navy. Pratt was supposed to be a very good commercial art school. After the Navy, I called Pratt, and they were full. Before going into the service, Jimmy Stevenson, who had gone to Cooper Union, had talked about that school. I called Cooper Union, and I had one or two days to file an application for a competitive test. I didn't want to go to the Art Students League, because it sounded too bohemian. Seventeen or eighteen hundred people took the test, and Cooper took ninety out of the crowd that year. I was pleasantly surprised when I got in. I remember sitting at a table with eight guys during the sculpture test. I was aware of Picasso and could have done that, but I decided to do a young man with a D.A. haircut, slightly twisted. The other guys were all doing flashy pieces.

When I got to Cooper Union, I was additionally surprised to find that two thirds of the class had been to Cooper Union night school or to art prep schools like Music and Art. Very few came out of the woods. I think this was a turning point in my life. I was at a tremendous disadvantage going into the school. I thought if I got in, I would work hard. I felt awful about myself at this point for having wasted so much time in the past, doing everything half-assed. I looked at myself. Number one: I had no good study habits. Number two: I was having a hard time catching up with what the teachers were talking about. And, number three: I knew I couldn't go out with the guys drinking beer at night, back in Queens.

But, everything at Cooper Union was exciting. The students were lively and diversified. I had always felt quite bizarre in Queens. At Cooper, I felt normal. I didn't feel weird anymore. The only things I had any security about were that I thought I could draw well, and I thought I could letter well. I had had a lot of experience drawing because of my job experience. I thought I knew lettering. In both, I found I was very wanting. I had done no fast drawing from life, only slow drawing. And the first time I lettered in class, my teacher, Nathaniel Farmer, told me I was going to have a terrible time in his class. He was right. Lettering is like abstract drawing, I found out. He had a nice set of hard standards. I think I did double the amount of work required. He said, "You worked very hard, but you haven't had childbirth yet: C."

The whole year was very lively. Art History was very interesting, but I couldn't figure it out. I didn't have enough background. But the teacher exempted me from the final because of the shape of my head. I was in pegged pants then. The class broke up over the shape of my head and my "genius."

In that first year, I was working on a plaster statue of a boxer. I had worked in the Jamaica Arena selling peanuts. They held boxing and wrestling matches there. The statue looked like it was made in Russia for the World's Fair. I must have used 159 lbs. of plaster in it, and half of it got carried everywhere. I was a menace in the school. The maintenance men were chasing me all over.

In the summer of the first year, I had the "52-20" G.I. Bill. I knew at that point, if I wanted to be a commercial artist, I should get a job in the field. I stayed home instead and painted six hours a day, five days a week. On Saturdays, I went out and played ball with my friends in the neighborhood. I lived at home in Queens. Cooper Union was being rebuilt that summer and didn't open on time, so I spent about four months painting every weekday, six hours a day. I don't know what I did on Sunday. I don't think I painted. I tried to handle the time like a job. But it seemed like there was something essentially wrong about painting every day and calling it work.

One of the paintings I spent a lot of time on was a music painting, squares with a piano player in it. I liked Mondrian's *Broadway Boogie Woogie*, and I liked boogie-woogie music, too. So, I wanted a painting like his with a piano player in it. I worked very hard. It was awful, but I didn't know how awful it was. I worked like a donkey and threw all the paintings out. My painting that summer was like the lettering class — a lot of work but very little accomplished.

The second year at Cooper Union, I went into advertising and wanted to take courses to broaden my range. So I took sculpture instead of some graphics courses, which didn't interest me much. We all took painting. The programs between fine art and commercial art weren't very different. I had had so much fun in sculpture the year before that I wanted to continue. I think this was the beginning of the end of commercial art.

I had Peter Busa for design, who was pretty exciting. And I had the same lettering teacher again. I wanted to change my program, but I said, "The hell with it" and stayed with him. Advanced Lettering. I started to figure what it was all about. The whole world was exploding for me. The design teacher showed me some Miró, and I got all the books I could find on Miró in the libraries, which were two.

I went to see Busa's shows. He was really avant-garde at the time. His paintings were like Indian blankets. He used bright dissonant colors, which I liked. He got bad reviews. One said they looked like a lot of brightly colored worms.

When one went into Cooper at that time, they encouraged you to paint in tasty, subdued colors. That got boring very quickly. I liked Busa's colors. The thing I wanted to do then was put two colors together, which would offend Busa but please me. He liked offensive, bright colors of his own taste. My painting got very good that year for an art student.

At night we went to hear a lot of Dixieland, which was around that year. There were Dixieland concerts that went up the Hudson at night during the summer, and I made a lot of drawings of the musicians. That summer, I painted with the same routine as the summer before. I did a jazz musician that I kept, without the Mondrian squares.

By now, I had real violent likes and dislikes in paintings in general and in the students' paintings. And, I decided to broaden my base further, which could be accomplished by dropping commercial art entirely. So I studied sculpture, painting, creative design, public speaking, and contemporary literature. I was playing basketball for Cooper Union every Saturday night. I liked everything that year, and I was more relaxed than the first two years, but I was getting to the point where I didn't want to go to school anymore.

I got a scholarship to study art in a school for the summer. Actually, Morris Kantor gave it to me. He thought it would be nice to spend a summer painting outdoors, and I chose Skowhegan. The next year, Skowhegan gave me a return scholarship. The first summer at Skowhegan, I still never thought I'd make a living as a fine artist. So I thought I'd do commercial art for money and paint the rest of the time. After I got out of Skowhegan that summer, I wanted to paint full time, despite the stories of deprivation, which was pretty much the case in those days.

Later, I was offered the possibility of going to Yale to get a degree. Josef Albers had left Black Mountain College and gone to Yale and asked Cooper Union for names of good students for the Yale art department for degrees. I thought it would be a pointless waste of time since this was after I had graduated from Cooper Union. It was 1950. By this time, I was already painting for a couple of years, and I didn't want to stop for anything.

William King in his studio on East Tenth Street, New York, 1954

WILLIAM KING

November 11, 1974

William King, that's my name. My father's name: Walter Blake King. My mother's name: Florence Dickey King. Her maiden name's my middle name. William Dickey King. My grandfather's name: William Dickey. I have a brother four years older than me: Walter Blake King, Jr. He is called Blake King.

Yes. The Kings. Georgia. My mother's from Pennsylvania, and her folks were just sort of petit bourgeois lumber dealers. I imagine there was a streak of romanticism going through them, like any mid-nineteenth-century Americans, a flaky humor — Mark Twain. I think it's sort of like a Russian story or Grimm's fairy tale. These five brothers had the lumber business, and they were all supposed to take care of some part of the action, and the guy who was supposed to take care of the insurance filed the notice in the desk. The lumberyard burned down, they were two days late with the insurance, so they all had to pack and scatter. Their business was shot, and they were disgraced.

My mother's father moved to South Carolina to do lumbering when he was a tiny kid, and it was like moving under a cloud, because it was all or half farms, not forests. And it was all downhill, because my grandfather didn't know anything but lumbering. Anyway, he then decided the best thing to do was raise chickens in Georgia.

We lived in Georgia, having moved from Florida, the better part of one year in the early 1930s — 1932, I think. I guess everything was really bad, and we went there to be able, really, to eat. My grandfather had the chicken farm. We had enough relatives around, but I didn't like it. I like the sea. I like the ocean. I feel trapped when I get inland. I like to be by the ocean. Florida. And New York is by the sea, too. It's the sea. You can smell it. You can see the gulls.

My father's family was from Georgia from 1600, something like that. And his mother was assaulted by the Yankees while she was burying the silverware. You know, Sherman going through Georgia. My mother said that's what made my father so crazy, because his mother was still angry at the Yankees.

I was born in Jacksonville, Florida, November 25, 1925. And moved progressively down the East Coast where my father was a civil engineer. He worked for Pan American Airways, so we wound up in Miami. Miami is a hybrid, not like a southern town. In those days, about sixty percent of the newcomers to Miami would be from Georgia, and the rest would be Jewish, from New York. Try to run a city like that. A lot were rednecks, and the rest were sort of sophisticated, more or less refugees. More sophisticated than those crackers.

It was an ex-boom town. Everybody had been going down there since 1918 or 1920, all the people who wanted to escape the north in winter. And there were two tall buildings out in the swamp. Still, it was pretty rural in the 1930s. And we lived in an even more country place, Coconut Grove. I'm not sure, but I think it was older than Miami. Anyway, people from Coconut Grove were snotty about people coming from Miami and even more so about the ones who lived at Coral Gables. Coconut Grove was started by some renegade college professor. And now, Coconut Grove is a real interface, because all the service industry people — workers, blacks, and the poor — came to live there, just divided by a railroad track from the rest.

In our house in Florida, there were a couple of rugs my mother had that might be thought of as art but mostly there were portable things. The house was unfinished. It was yellow pine inside and creosote on the outside. There were a lot of houses like that in Florida. I think it was sort of nomad decor. I guess my mother had things that meant something to her personally: personal-ware. A couple of odd doodads, a blue bowl, some silverware. It was very, very Arabic; all moveable. Not much interest in durable goods. There was an icebox, a kerosene stove, things like that that couldn't be moved, but that's about it.

When I was little, I was in this private school. My mother was a schoolteacher, and she got a job at the Elsie K. Poe Outdoor School for Boys and Girls. We went to school in these two thatched shacks right on the beach, and we'd go swimming every day. It was terrific. I was put in the Coconut Grove Elementary School in the first grade. They took me there in the morning, and the first day, at lunchtime, I showed up at home. I didn't like it. They couldn't keep me there. They couldn't make me stay there.

So my mother put me in this other school. There was probably nobody in the third grade. All grades were in the same room, and they needed a third grader, I guess. There were no windows in the school, just storm shutters — you open them up and put a stick to hold them up. If there were too many mosquitoes, we couldn't have school, and everybody stayed home. If there were high tides, like in October, we had no school. There were two cars. My mother drove one, Mrs. Poe, the other, and they picked up the kids.

There were about a dozen kids — "cases," I suppose we were — in the whole school. It was really neat, except that all the other kids went to public schools, tough schools, and you felt peculiar going to this one: hot-house types, I guess. It went up through the seventh grade.

Then I had to go to Coral Gables Elementary. Oy! I remember that. A horrible, great big thing. I went there for the eighth grade, and that's when I started feeling odd, peculiar, and getting all these pimples. Hideous. I'm laughing, but I was miserable. I was always in love, unrequited. I just loved beautiful girls. I was the toad prince or something. Then I went to junior high school. That was worse. That was horrible, just horrible. I didn't like high school, either, except for the band.

In early school, I did nothing at all related to sculpture. When I was off from school, when I was little, we played in the woods all around us, or in the rock pit: tag, alligator — kids' games. But building airplane models, that was the thing.

Very early, I used different materials and did things with them. We had a shop, and my father always had a lot of tools. My father built the house we lived in, mostly. He was a great improviser, to my mother's dismay. He built a lot of things — temporary things — and they're still there, forty years later. And I think he would do things in an unorthodox way, partly out of frustration at not being educated. He was a very handy person and a self-taught civil engineer. And I bet that's where I got unorthodox ideas about how to stick things together or how and what to use if you don't have something you want.

But, it's his personality, too. My mother said that before Christmas one time, my brother wanted to wrap presents and had a fit because there wasn't any wrapping paper, and that I got out the crayons and made some. I'm nervous talking about the next one. The other thing she said was that she took the car keys by mistake, and I had to go to band rehearsal in the car, and I found an old key, and I remembered the shape of the car key and filed it out. I filed it from memory. I started the car with the damn key — didn't think much about it. Desperate, something's got to be done.

I'm going to tell you about the first sculpture I ever made. I never told anybody this. It's gross, but it's touching. I made a little figure out of plasticine — I don't know where I got the modeling clay — and I copied this little female figure that I could hold in my hand, and I'd look at it and masturbate. I was about ten or eleven years old. So that's it. And I think that's where I got started.

It's funny, later the material would dictate the form, the imagery. I don't know, it's got a life of its own. I tried — when I was at Berkeley teaching for a year, many years later — to make some California sculpture. It was very impressive, the things they were doing out there — far out. I tried to make some things that were appropriate to being there, and they just died. So I kept doing those shapes the way they came out. I didn't argue with it.

I grew up there in Coral Gables. I was supposed to be an engineer. I went to the University of Florida. My brother had gone there. My father was an engineer, my brother's an engineer, I was supposed to be an engineer. I skipped the last year in high school — that was 1941 or 1942 — because if I went to engineering school, I wouldn't be drafted. Both my father and brother were in the army, and they said, "Forget it." I guess I was sort of a sissy, and they thought I would succumb if I went into the army. Jesus! So, I took the entrance exam, and instead of taking the last year of high school, I went up there. I've regretted it ever since. The last year of high school is the year you just coast and have a nice time. I used to play in the band in high school, a dance band. I played saxophone. It was a lot of fun, and now it was all over.

We'd play big band music, the Glenn Miller–type thing. It was a lot of fun. Towards the end of my junior year, the guys who were in the band in the last year of high school graduated, left. They had a really good band so we took most of the jobs they would do. We'd play at the Coconut Grove movie house on Saturday afternoon, the Mickey Mouse show. After the movie, the curtain would part and there we were, we'd be playing away. The kids would come out and do amateur turns. We'd get paid in passes. And we played at the R.A.F. tea dances at the University of Miami. England had this R.A.F. group — trainees — there. We had the same group to play for them. We played written music, charts, like any damn dance band.

In 1945, I was deported to New York. My mother gave me a hundred bucks and she said, "You'd better get out of town. This place is no good for anyone over sixteen and under sixty-five. Nothing's happening here, so if you've got any brains, you'll leave." I ran away to New York — kind of — with a girl I met when I was working at Pan American Airways.

There were three reasons my mother thought I should go to New York. The first was that she told me my father would lean over my brother's crib when he was a tiny baby, saying, "You're going to be an engineer. You're going to be an engineer." He is an engineer, and he hates it. He should have been a preacher or a musician. That's where his heart is. And I think she saw that happening to my brother, and she said, "It isn't going to happen to the other one."

She gave me so many choices it damn near drove me nuts. She told me that she'd put out three little short pants on the bed, little shirts, and three pairs of socks, and say, "Okay, now choose." She would say, "You've got to make your own choice." It turns out, later, whenever I've got to make a choice, I start blubbering, but I do it. So, I think that was one thing about sending me to New York.

Another one was, I think she wanted to get a divorce from my father, and she couldn't do it while I was around. She kept saying, "I've got to get out from under. I've got to get out from under. I'm going to wait until you kids grow up. I'm going to get out of here, and I'm going to get out from under." So, that was another reason I was sent off.

I guess the main reason was she knew there were more chances in New York. I'm sure she thought I was talented, but in what way, I don't know. But if something was going to happen, it probably was going to happen up there. It wasn't going to happen in Florida.

There was a girl who was always telling me about the big city. We were patching up these big airplanes at Dinner Key [Marina, Coconut Grove]. Pan American had seaplanes. That was during the war [World War Two]. They still flew them around, and they'd land in the water and run into sticks and have little holes and big holes, and we'd patch them. So Gerry — that's her — she'd go on about New York all the time. It came to pass that she said she was going back to New York, and I said I was going to California to study architecture at U.C.L.A., but I'd sure like to go up north and see the big city first.

So, my mother gave me a hundred bucks, like I said, and sure enough, one day in June, 1945, we got on the train and went to New York. We got off in New York, and I couldn't believe it. Big buildings, people in overcoats and hats — it was early June and still kind of chilly. We came in through New Jersey. We could see the Empire State Building — that was fine! And the ground was shaking, and Penn Station was like the Baths of Caracalla with a glass top, beautiful. That was two days before a plane flew into the Empire State Building — a bomber flew into it!

I took a room in the Sloan House Y.M.C.A. I couldn't stand those tiger cages. So I said, "How's about let's get a place and live?" So Gerry and I got a place, a furnished flat on 110th or 112th Street, and I took a job for the summer, still intending to go to California.

She said, "There's this terrific place, Cooper Union." I thought, "Union? I don't want a union." I wanted to join the musicians' union, though, in New York. I took my union card from Florida — because I had played in a big band in Florida — to the 802 office. The guy says, "Defunct local. Okay, six hundred bucks initiation fee." So I didn't join the union.

But I took a drafting job and the entrance exam for Cooper Union. I don't know why, because I wasn't going to stay. And I was sick. I had a sore throat. I had pimples. I had a fever. I had postnasal drip. But I took it. They told me later I got the highest mark of anybody who ever took it, except for drawing. I almost flunked that. So they said I was accepted, but I didn't want that. I wasn't going to stay. Then, the summer wore on and on, and I decided I didn't want to go. I didn't want to go to California. I wanted to stay in New York with Gerry. So, I thought I'd go to Columbia instead and study architecture.

I wrote to my aunt in Atlanta, Aunt Mildred, who was always saying, "Can I help? Can I help? Can I help? What do you want to do? You two kids are all I've got." So I said, "I want to borrow ninety bucks to pay the tuition at Columbia Architecture School for a year." Great. I waited about a week, the ninety bucks didn't show up. It was August, and I was saving everything I could from this stupid drafting job. Gerry and I moved to a furnished place on Perry Street in Greenwich Village for about a month. It was awful. The first night we were there, we began to itch. That's the first time in my life I'd ever seen a bed bug. I just about went out of my gourd. We got up in the middle of the night, scratching and cursing, and put on our clothes and got the Ninth Street crosstown bus to the Valencia Hotel. It's still there, a home away from home. I called the renting agent, and he said, "We'll have the exterminators there first thing in the morning, Sir."

That ninety dollars. That's the funniest thing. It came like this: I wired my aunt and said, "I've got to register three days from now. If you're going to send me the ninety bucks, this is it. Now or never." She sent a check, and where it said [the amount] in numbers, it said, "$9.00," and where it said it in words, it said, "Ninety." So I couldn't cash it. I was beside myself. I didn't know what the hell to do. And then Gerry said, "Why don't you go to Cooper Union? You've been accepted." I said, "It's free. It's a junky-assed school, down there in the Bowery." But the next day school started so I went there.

The first day of the first class was [Sidney] Delavante's drawing class, where you draw all day, one of the few all-day classes of the foundation courses. And he said, "All right, everybody, go downstairs and buy a newsprint pad and charcoal." (And come back and draw this jerk in a clown's suit.) I had never done any drawing, no charcoal, newsprint. What was this? And it hit me halfway through the first hour: This is school? This is fun. I hated school. So I thought, this is all right. So I went back the next day and the next day and the next day.

Halfway through the term, I decided I wanted to be a sculptor. I wrote to my brother and told him. I didn't write my mother or my aunt, because I had already come down from being an engineer. I thought they were going to make me come back and work in a gas station.

When I was in Cooper Union, I stayed with Gerry at first. We weren't married, and she was a few years older than me. She was embarrassed, and she got worried about not being married. I think she wanted to get married. Not to me, to somebody. She was getting on — all of twenty-five, maybe twenty-six, or something like that. We were on 7th Street on Avenue C, a nice flat. Seven bucks a month.

Very nice, Polish, Ukrainian neighborhood. We were entertaining other Cooper students, and I guess they were shocked. Anyway, it wasn't good, so I got an apartment with two classmates, Bill Hanes and Jimmy Moon, on 9th Street and Second Avenue, and I stayed there the rest of the time I was at Cooper Union. We don't see much of each other anymore. She got married, had a couple of kids. She married some old guy. He had a toilet seat factory, and then he went into making furs.

I didn't like any courses much at Cooper Union, besides sculpture. The thing about Cooper Union was, the veterans were coming back after 1945. That was a vintage year. A lot of people coming in who were out for so many years brought an adult attitude. They were serious, impatient. They were not going to be treated like children at all. That was the atmosphere there, and I felt pretty much like a kid.

I know now that the students were nourished by each other. They were people of a certain age, all in the same boat in that time, 1945 to 1948, a revolutionary period in American art. There was no American art, nothing. Nothing until 1948 when the New York School — de Kooning and all those guys — all of a sudden got some attention. And all of a sudden, we got some American art. Before that, it was Paris. It was mind-bending. A mind-bending time to be thinking about being an American artist. Just like being reborn, not once, coming out of school, but twice. All of a sudden, you're in the world instead of just out in the sticks.

So that was the atmosphere, and I knew I was good, and I knew I had talent, but I was so screwed up, I couldn't deal with any people. With inanimate things, objects, materials I could say something, but with the other students, boy, it was not good.

I went to the dean's office, because I'd kept a book out of the library three months too long. Dean Vaughan said, "Now, it's just a book, don't get so —" I must have been sitting under a table or something, destroyed with guilt. And he was saying, "We have this psychologist here from Payne Whitney, and I think you'd better make an appointment." I don't know whether I was jibbering or what. So I didn't feel so good at school, except for art. Most of the courses I thought were a crock.

Delavante took us to the Buchholz Gallery early on, in the first year, 1945, to a David Smith show. Curt Valentin and Mary Willard had galleries on the same floor, I think it was 2 West 57th Street. And they had this big David Smith show. There was a girl in Delavante's class named Dorothy Kessler, an intellectual. A great big girl. I mean, very wide, tall, and tough. I liked her a lot. We used to talk a lot, have lunch. So, she's up there at the David Smith show with the rest of the drawing class, and she looked at one of the sculptures and says, "Just like modern music." And starts hammering on it: Boing, boing, boing!

Bang! Clang! And the dealer, Curt Valentin, he just chewed her out to pieces. She was in tears in about two seconds. And I said, "Don't cry, I'll make you one."

I went back to school, and I had this piece of brass, and I was sawing that with a hacksaw, putting it together with screws. It was a person, and I gave it to her. I was making it after school, and my sculpture teacher, [Dikran] Dingilian, comes in and says, "What's that you're making?" I said, "That's a statue." He said. "That's pretty good." He started to leave and turned around and said, "You know, I bet you could sell that. I bet you could get fifty bucks for that."

After Cooper Union, I went to Skowhegan and later had a Fulbright to Italy. Italy sort of beefed up my resolve to be an artist. When I look back, I see that's what happened. Lois [Dodd] and I got married after I came back from Skowhegan. I got this scholarship for the summer, and I didn't want to not go. That seemed like the most important thing, and so I went. Came back and got married in October. We went to Sag Harbor on our honeymoon. We lived on 29th Street over the winter, and I found a studio, some storefront. Lois went out and did textile designs, tie designs.

Dean [Dana P.] Vaughan of Cooper called one day and said, "There's some woman artist here that's got too much work to do on the *S.S. United States*, and she's looking for somebody, a graduate, to help out." So that's how I got to do the piece. She came around to 29th Street and had some sketches of the project she had in mind for the first-class smoking room. She said she had too much else to do, needed somebody, younger, I guess, and Vaughan recommended me. So I made a sketch for it, and they loved it. I got Rambusch Decorating Company to construct it. It looked like something that belonged in a boat, brass and blue and shiny. The Rambusch Company was on 13th Street, and they did all that. They did some beautiful automats. So they made the thing, put it on the boat, and I went to see it. I went on the boat to England later. That's commercial art. But sure, it gave me a lot of confidence. I guess I figured I could cut it after that. I know there's a lot of sweating and fear of the unknown, but I guess I never really . . . You know, it's funny, Eli [King, his son] says a lot of things like, "How could you come to New York at twenty and get a job and do all that stuff like that?" And I keep telling him, "Listen, Eli, I had asthma, my knees were knocking, I had pimples, I didn't know what the fuck I was doing."

I had to get in there. I had to get on, you know. I had to get out on the floor. New York was the school, the university. This is it.

Philip Pearlstein in midtown New York City, summer 1949

PHILIP PEARLSTEIN

March 2, 1975

I was born in Pittsburgh in 1924. I was an only child. My father was born in Pittsburgh, but my mother came here, when she was nine or ten, from Lithuania. My mother's was sort of a Cinderella-type story. She had three older brothers in Lithuania, and her mother died, when she was still young, from gangrene. My mother's older brother had gone to a fortune teller, who had told him that his mother was going to die in a very short time. And his mother died in a very short time. His father — my grandfather — remarried. His new wife was a shrewish woman, who was always beating up my mother — who must have been five or six — using her as a housemaid, knocking her front teeth out in anger one day.

The way my mother told it, that was the precipitating incident for the brothers to immigrate to America. Her oldest brother came over first and got a job, and sent for the others, including my mother. First they were in the food business in Brooklyn, out on Flatbush Avenue somewhere. Then they went to Pittsburgh. My father was in the food business, too. He grew up in Pittsburgh. They were in chickens and eggs and fish. I guess my father went to work for her brothers. That's how they met.

I have an early memory of a house we lived in. Probably a single-family house, where we lived on the first floor. I slept on a folding cot. My parents owned the house and rented out the second floor as a separate apartment. Two of my mother's brothers owned houses in the same row of houses, which were fairly new. My father's family lived across the street in a bigger, older house. My father's father died at an early age, leaving my father's mother with a family of eight children. My father was the eldest, so he had the role of being the head of the family. His youngest sister was only eight or nine years older than me. My five uncles were trolley car ticket collectors when they were young and taxi cab drivers when older; one later became a telegraph operator and another became a clerk in a drugstore, as did my youngest aunt. My other aunt became a secretary. They lived diagonally across the street from our house, so I grew up with young aunts and uncles. Also, each of my mother's brothers had two or three children. Even though I was an only child, I was hardly ever alone. We had constant gatherings. My father was an organizer, and on weekends we used to go off on picnics, riding in the back of my mother's family's business truck. The families would make up big bundles, baskets of food — meat roasts, roast chickens, that was the big thing — and go off to the public parks: South Park in Pittsburgh, North Park beyond McKeesport. They'd set up a string of tables, and it would be like an old fashioned reunion, every weekend in summer. One of my earliest paintings was of this scene, with all my aunts and uncles and cousins.

The house we lived in was pretty small. I used to build things with an erector set, which took up a lot of room. My father's whole family grew up a-culturally. The only thing I got from them was reading *Doc Savage* magazines. I copied the illustrations. My memories are vague about school in the primary grades. Mostly I remember my cousins at that time.

I remember one boy I became friendly with. We lived in a section of Pittsburgh called the Hill District, which is now all black. Back then it was half Jewish, half black. My friend, Harold Hirsch, who became an architect, was the son of the owner of the dry cleaning store, so his family was a notch higher on the social scale and was interested in going to museums. We would walk over a steep hill, cutting through some wilderness, past a huge cemetery, down into the valley where the skyscraper that was to become the University of Pittsburgh was under construction. We would walk through the steel beam foundation structure to get to the Carnegie Museum. We just wandered around.

The big traumatic experience of the time was the start of the Depression. My mother's brother's business collapsed. At some point, her eldest brother moved back to New York with his family. He had married a girl from New York City, so they had a family in New York. My uncle later came back alone and moved in with us, because things were apparently very bad in New York. He started his own little business, which eventually became very successful.

At about this time, my father was out of work again. He had been working for a big meat packing house in Pittsburgh that went bankrupt, and my father got a job in another packing house in Wheeling, West Virginia. I guess I was ten. We moved to Wheeling, into a real slum area. This was the first time I had to make friends all by myself. The neighborhood kids thought we were strange as we were the only Jews in the area, sort of exotic.

In Wheeling, it was the first time I was aware of being Jewish. We were never religious, but my father was the only Jew working in that packing company, and I was the only Jewish kid in the public school. Somehow, everybody knew it, and so I felt very outside. But, I was one of the bigger kids, I had grown up fast. In those days I was one of the taller kids in my class.

The house we moved into was built over an old mine. The floor boards were all rotted, and when we moved in, the movers put down a heavy piece of furniture and it went through the floor. I remember my mother crying. The house was built on a steep hillside, and you'd walk up the hill through dense woods, climbing up the roots of trees, just hanging on. Then, over the other side, it was barren.

We lived right near a stockyard and also a china dish company dumping ground. And I remember going with a new friend on summer afternoons, searching through the dumping ground. We found usable things. The area was also surrounded by woods, which I found exciting.

I remember fishing in a stream with our hands. There was one spot where the fish were so dense in the water you could just reach down and grab one. They were probably just catfish. There was a crowd of people grabbing fish, which they took home to eat. My new friend, Frank Kloss, showed me Indian caves, where there were Indian glyphs on the walls. This made a tremendous impression on me. When I was painting expressionist landscapes later, I recalled the feeling of those caves.

In Wheeling I used to walk railroad tracks with my friend Frank. In Wheeling we also used to walk to a big amusement park on an island in the Ohio River. My first serious artwork started in West Virginia, in the classroom in Wheeling. We stayed there until that packing house went bankrupt, and we went back to Pittsburgh. After we moved back to Pittsburgh when I was eleven or twelve, we moved into a house with all my father's brothers and sisters and my grandmother, and all these people shared three bedrooms. I shared a bedroom with my grandmother and two aunts.

That is the time when my interest in making art picked up. It was strange. This family was not cultured, but my father's youngest sister and youngest brother did go to the theater. They had jobs as sales clerks in a downtown drug store. My aunt took me to the theater a couple of times. I became very interested in stage design, and I made my own miniature theater. Looking back, I can't remember where I picked up the information, but I was involved in building a stage to scale, with a lighting system, and designing shows with miniature sets. One of my uncles one night burned down my stage. The house was very small, and my tabletop theater took up too much space, but I have had mixed feelings about my uncles ever since. They also used my fish bowl of guppies for a spittoon. Anyways, the miniature theater stage somehow led to my real involvement in art.

Though not religious, my father had me study with an Orthodox rabbi, who'd come around once a week. My miniature theater was on a folding bridge table, which was set up all week. It was a little living room. I mean, I can understand my uncle's urge to get rid of it — it took up a good part of the space. I would have to strip everything off it and have my Hebrew lesson. And I remember having a Bar Mitzvah ceremony in a storefront synagogue.

Anyway, the next year — I must have been in the eighth grade — my father became a huckster, selling groceries, chickens, and fish from the back of his Model T Ford, which he made into a truck. Maybe by this time it wasn't a Model T, but the rumble seat became his truck.

The Depression had eased up by this time. My parents and I moved into a small apartment of our own, and I had my own bedroom. My theater grew. Movies like *Marie Antoinette* with Norma Shearer and Tyrone Power impressed me, and I made my own mini-version of parts of Versailles with miniature figures made of balsa wood. I did research and made authentic costumes that were more glued than sewn together. Then I spent most of the time playing around with the lights. I got involved with a couple of other students, who were also interested in theater, but I was the only one who had gone so far as making the model sets.

One of those friends was Martin Friedman, who is now the director of The Walker Art Center [Friedman served as director from 1961 until his retirement in 1990]. Actually, my first painting came about because he and I were taking a walk on a summer night in a park near our neighborhood in Pittsburgh past a merry-go-round, which was closed and boarded up, and we began to make up a play about a murder at the carousel. I was going to do a miniature stage set of a carousel, and for the first time it just seemed such a chore that I made a painting of it. That really got me interested in painting. About a year later, that painting won first prize in oil painting in the annual National Scholastic High School Art Contest, and the year after that, I won a prize again with the painting I mentioned earlier of the family picnic.

The same year the carousel won the prize for oil painting, I also had a painting in watercolor of a black barbershop that won the prize for watercolor. The two award winners were in a show that circulated and eventually went to the Metropolitan Museum and was written up by *Life* magazine. My two paintings were reproduced. The carousel painting took up half the page, and the barbershop took up another quarter of the page. Someone else's painting was reproduced next to my barbershop. And the over-page had about nine small color reproductions of others' paintings. It was a big number. I got the big play. I became a local celebrity. This was overwhelming to my uncles, who had been treating me as some sort of freak. That convinced me to be an artist and gave me a future.

I should have mentioned the Saturday morning art classes. From the eighth grade on, I attended Saturday morning painting classes at the Carnegie Museum. I met a lot of young people there, including my fellow artist friends from my high school. It became a whole social life.

One of the teachers at the Saturday morning classes was Sam Rosenberg, Pittsburgh's great "old master" of painting. His son, who was my age, was also in the Saturday morning classes, and I got to know him pretty well. He eventually became a doctor, but back then Mr. Rosenberg had been teaching his son an old-master painting technique, glazing oil paint colors over an egg tempera underpainting, and his son initiated me into that procedure, which became my way of painting.

From the tenth grade on, I was in the classes of a terrific art teacher in my Pittsburgh high school, the Taylor Allderdice High School. The teacher's name was Joe Fitzpatrick. Eventually he became the superintendent of art in the Pittsburgh high schools. He created a tremendous sense of excitement about art. He was a tall, handsome, sophisticated type. He was extremely charming. He dressed immaculately. He was very proud of the way he looked, of his clothes, yet somehow did not seem vain. And the excitement he generated about art was genuine.

He held an art club in his classroom every day after school hours. There must have been about eighteen of us who gathered there to work on our own projects. It really became a way of life. Unfortunately for my education, I went through high school totally ignorant. I mean, we — the art group — would get totally involved with very elaborate stage productions that the high school graduating classes would put on. Of course, those of us working on the stage sets had to have time off our classes, so I never went to algebra, or any of such courses — history, languages — which I miss now.

But then it was really terrific. It was the only glamour any of us experienced. And we helped put on fantastic productions. In my junior year in high school, the seniors put on a tremendous musical with Gene Kelly there, directing. There were a dozen or more stage sets, costume changes, and the whole thing was a super-glamorous experience. That must have been in 1941.

From that group there are ten or twelve who are still very much involved in art. Andy Warhol was a student in classes Joe Fitzpatrick taught in another school, a few years later. So the guy absolutely was dynamic and had a magical touch. For instance, besides myself, in our group there was Martin Freidman, who became a museum director; and Erwin Kalla, who is now a big designer of paper products and luggage produced in Japan — almost all the paper products in household goods stores seen now are designed by him. Another fellow, who really was the most brilliant and talented of the group, Lee Goldman, became an industrial designer. He worked for Corning-

Steuben Glass, and was for a time the head of their design program. Later he was head of the art department of Carnegie Tech. Another fellow, Stuart Williams, is an executive with one of the bigger advertising companies. A girl named Joan Seigfried is an art historian. Her greatest public contribution so far was a show of comic book–influenced art. It traveled around for a couple of years. She teaches at Skidmore [College]. Sidney Simon is a nationally known sculptor and a founder of the Skowhegan summer art school in Maine. Some of the other people remained in Pittsburgh and are prominent in the art scene there; a fellow named Jerry Kaplan is head of the art department at Chatham College. It was a very exciting high school experience, capped by the reproductions of my painting in *Life* magazine.

A number of us went on to Carnegie Institute of Technology to the art department. By the year after my freshman year, a whole group of us were in the army. I think the reproduction of my paintings in *Life* magazine was in 1941, so I think I went into the army in 1943, at the end of freshman year.

At Carnegie Tech, during the freshman year, I became friendly with Fred Mitchell. Though I won first prizes for two years in the National Scholastic High School Contests, what I really wanted that they awarded was a scholarship. But I got first prize instead. Mitchell got the scholarship. He came from Mississippi, so he won the scholarship, and I was very envious of him. The tuition then was about $300 for the year, but that was beyond my family's possibilities. Carnegie Tech gave me a half scholarship. I guess I still owe them $150.

Fred Mitchell was a terrific influence in his own way, like Fitzpatrick. He was the most sophisticated, most knowledgeable kid in the class, who knew all about classical music, symphonies, all about van Gogh. Extraordinarily charming. He was very romantic looking in those days. Very thin. Anyway, he got me and several others involved in things we never bothered with before. We went to concerts and knew all about van Gogh and El Greco, whom I'd never heard of before. We'd go to movies at the art movie house. Generally he served as a catalyst, and a group of us gathered around him. Probably any group at college has this sudden expansion of horizons.

Then the war came, and we all went off and joined it. The *Life* magazine article became my passport within the United States Army. At the interview, when I was first inducted, I showed the interviewer the copy of *Life* magazine I brought with me. Of course it was overwhelming to him. You can imagine the effect of a kid opening the magazine to that page of reproductions.

So, I took infantry training. We were scheduled to be infantry casualty replacements. Almost everybody I was trained with became replacements in the battles, those beach landings in Italy. A few of us were instead sent to an infantry training camp in Florida, where I was put to work with a group of men who had been commercial artists and were now assigned to producing visual training aids, charts of weapons — how to use them, how to take them apart for cleaning and put them back together, care and maintenance of equipment, how to read maps, etc. There was silkscreening set up for reproducing the charts in multiples. It was fantastic art training for me.

At that point I was nineteen, and I was working with older men who had a lot of experience in the commercial art field. They were mostly from the West Coast. They taught me a lot about lettering and perspective — I mean *more* about them, I already knew something — and organization, design, and page layout, and how to cut the stencils for the screens and mix the colors. I worked along with the others in the actual mechanical work of silkscreen printing.

So while all the men I had trained with were having horrendous experiences, I had this great art training. That lasted about eight months, then the army decided that those of us who had these nice jobs had to be sent overseas and our jobs given to people who had been overseas. The unit was broken up, and I was given basic infantry training all over again. I was shipped to Italy, to an infantry replacement camp nicknamed the "Dairy Farm Repple Depple" [a G.I. term for "replacement depot"]. The battle of Monte Cassino had just ended, and this place was in the area. We took more training around there. That's when I first got to Naples, and, on different weekends, went to Capri, to Sorrento, and saw Pompeii. I drew all the time.

Back in Florida, working in the training aid shop, I had a lot of free time, so I had done a series of watercolors, which were ambitious, which I still have. I was thinking then of becoming an illustrator, and I was building up my portfolio. I would get criticism from the artists I worked with, but it was obvious that I was way beyond them. But they discussed the work with me in a professional way that was very nice. In Italy I made dozens of small drawings, some of them carefully finished. And all of which I still have. Some of them are very ambitious. One day in that training center in Italy, I met up with one of the fellows from the unit in Florida. He had talked his way into setting up a sign painting shop there.

I got transferred to Rome, where the army was setting up a huge replacement training center to train everybody who had been in Africa or Italy, through those campaigns, who were no longer needed in their special fields, who were going to be trained as basic infantrymen for the big push out of the stalemate in the mountains above Florence. It was to chase the Germans up beyond the Alps. That meant that men who were lieutenants and captains and staff sergeants were taking training along with men like myself who were much younger and of lesser rank.

So I took the full basic infantry training course for the third time. A lot of the men I met at that point were really terrific. I mean, when you think of the army, you don't expect to find stage designers, opera singers, business executives, or contractors. The one I became most friendly with had studied opera singing and had been a literature major in college. He and the fellow who had been in stage design, and a couple of men who had been business executives, who thought of themselves as sophisticated, would rent a box at the Royal Opera in Rome once a week. This was the final winter of the war, but once a week we went to the opera. And it was just tremendous. I really learned a lot from these older men. There was a whole world beyond what I had known in Pittsburgh.

During the war in Italy, I had a great deal of freedom. I spent a lot of time in Italy after the war ended. I never got to combat, so I didn't have combat points that could get me home faster, so I was in Italy almost a full year after the war ended. That's when all the art was being brought out. Special exhibitions set up everywhere. So that year was great for me, giving me a kind of living art-history survey of Renaissance art.

Then the war experience ended for me. I came back to Pittsburgh. I had the G.I. Bill so I went back to college. That's where I met Dorothy [Cantor, later Pearlstein], Andy Warhol, and George Klauber. George had studied at Pratt Institute in New York before the war. He had come to Carnegie Tech just for one year. But in that year (like Fred Mitchell before) he got a group of us involved. Whereas, before the war, discovering Tchaikovsky was a big thing, after the war, with Klauber, it was Mahler, Schoenberg, Bartók. He was involved in abstraction. He really introduced us to modern art, to contemporary New York art. That was 1946 to '47. And we have remained close friends.

Because of the training I'd had with the commercial artists in Florida, I was hired by the professor who was head of the design program at Carnegie Tech, Robert Lepper, to work with him on a freelance job he had doing catalogs for architectural aluminum products, for ALCOA. He worked in an architect's office, and in collaboration with the architects he designed the catalogs. He needed somebody who could be a draftsman with some sensitivity to what he was doing. As I had come back from the army in late spring and my school year would not start until fall, I had five to six months free.

Lepper was a brilliant man who was completely into the Bauhaus idea. He had been a protégé of a man who had studied at the Bauhaus, named [Rowena Reed] Kostellow, who had just left Carnegie to start Pratt Institute's industrial design department. I worked very closely with Lepper that summer, and I continued that job for the next three years that I was at Carnegie Tech, working weekends and holidays. It was a different kind of exposure to ideas about art.

96

Before the war, the Carnegie Museum had held international shows of contemporary European art that I saw, and during the war years the museum did big American art shows. But I can't remember any particular painting that gave me a thrill.

When I was in Italy, in Rome, I had had the Vatican Museum at my disposal on weekends. Almost nobody else was there, and I could go into the Sistine Chapel and lie down on a bench and stay looking up at Michelangelo's ceiling as long as I wanted. It was incredible. And there were other exhibitions in Rome. One of the other paintings I remember most from that period was Velasquez's *Pope Innocent X*, which was in an exhibition of artworks that had been put away for safe keeping during the fighting and were now being exhibited in the Palazzo Venezia, in what had been Mussolini's offices. I remember being overwhelmed by that painting.

When I went back to Pittsburgh, I knew my stay would be temporary. I would have left as soon as I came out of the army, but as I was an only child, I felt an obligation to stay home for a couple of years. Let my parents look at me. There was no question of staying in Pittsburgh.

I was excited about the idea of visual training aids and thought of doing visual charts for public school education. During the last year at Carnegie, I worked out a project to present a visual study of the Constitution of the United States — or sections of it — to study the arguments about the ideas that were behind the writing of it, and then how it was supposed to work. And my army training aide experience went into that. I designed and illustrated an introductory booklet. I also wrote the text, counted the characters, and blocked out the text. So it was a complete "dummy," or could have been at that point, along with the illustrations I made. I picked on the Electoral College section and worked out its mechanism and demonstrated it in a series of charts, which I illustrated elaborately.

I came to New York with this thing on the United States Constitution. That was the main part of my portfolio when I arrived. That was the kind of thing I wanted to do. My arrival coincided with the beginning of the Joe McCarthy era. The art directors of the publications I showed this Constitution business to thought I was a political nut of some sort. They didn't see it in my terms, and suddenly all my ambitions had been wiped out. I was getting terribly depressed.

I came to New York with Andy Warhol, who had a brilliant portfolio of illustrations, and of course, by the end of the first week we were here, he had a terrific illustration job lined up. We lived together from June to March, 1950. Dorothy was a year behind us in college, and we had decided to get married when she graduated.

Andy and I came to New York in June 1949, living first in a small apartment on St. Mark's Place right off Avenue A that we sublet from friends of Balcomb Greene, who had been our professor of art history at Carnegie Tech and had encouraged us to move to New York. When that summer rental ended, we found a crazy place through an ad in *The New York Times*: the front room of a dance studio. It was an enormous loft, most of which was a dance theater with a proscenium arch at the far end behind which the dancer lived with her partner. There was a collection of marvelous primitive musical instruments.

Our landlady was the dancer Francesca Boas, who was the daughter of Franz Boas, the anthropologist. She and the woman who was her partner were renting out the big front room, and that's what Andy and I moved into. It was a very weird time there with these two women, which would make a nice short novel written by someone like Tennessee Williams. But it is where, with their help, Andy Warhola found himself as "Andy Warhol." Until then, he was a quiet, naive, shy kid with a nice sense of humor, who just did those brilliant illustrations and had all those terrific jobs lined up right away, while I was still hunting for a job.

My whole ambitious project just turned to shit, defeated by Joe McCarthy. And then our friend George Klauber, who by that time was well established as assistant to the art director of *Fortune* magazine, Will Burton, heard of a job as a production assistant to a famous graphic designer, who had arrived in the U.S. at the beginning of the war.

The designer's name was Ladislav Sutnar. He looked at my U.S. Constitution project and found it impressive, but he thought it was ugly. He was impressed with the fact that an art student would do it. He had been teaching at Pratt Institute. He was Czechoslovakian and had designed the Czech Pavilion for the 1939 World's Fair, and he had been sent here by the Nazis when they took over Czechoslovakia to sell off the materials, as the building had not yet been erected.

He had been friends with Maholy-Nagy and the whole Bauhaus group. His office was Serge Chermayeff's former office, which he took over when Chermayeff went off to Chicago to start the New Bauhaus there. In Czechoslovakia, he had been minister of culture and had established his own design school, state run. It was something like the Bauhaus, essentially an art trade school. So he looked at my portfolio as a teacher and saw the ambition of it and the fact that I had organized so much material into some sort of rational form. He hired me, on the basis of the catalogs I had worked on with Robert Lepper in Pittsburgh, to do drafting and paste-ups and, later, some lower-level designing.

I worked with him full-time, as well as part-time when I went back to school on the G.I. Bill at New York University for three years to study art history. [Pearlstein received his M.A. in 1955. His thesis was on Francis Picabia.] I worked with him for the next seven or eight years. In fact, practically until our son William was born. When he offered to make me a junior partner, I couldn't face that, and I left and went to work at *Life* magazine, where I did the same sort of work.

He was probably the biggest influence in my mature life. He was everything Lepper was intellectually, only on an international scale. In Europe, before the war, he'd been one of the founders of modern typography, important as a book, poster, and catalog designer, as well as an industrial designer and architect. In the United States, he had to start over again. He did a couple of books here, a book on catalog design, another on point-of-sale design, and another on package design, which had big circulation. They are still being sold. They are big in the art departments of colleges. I worked on those books and a bunch of other catalogs.

He is the one responsible for my studying art history. He was surprised when he first saw my portfolio, because of his experience with American art students, who he said wanted "the bubbles without the process of making the champagne." He said that at least I knew that you had to stamp on the grapes. But early on I found him to be a nervous wreck, and he would proceed to draw everyone around him into the same state; it was always a miserable emotional experience. He would storm and rage, doors would slam, things would get tossed around.

I felt that commercial art wasn't worth that kind of emotional energy. It wasn't for me. If every day was going to be that miserable, I might as well be a painter. And I began painting seriously. Then, as I still had some time on the G.I. Bill, I thought of studying art history. Some of our friends went to Paris on the G.I. Bill. But Mr. Sutnar encouraged me to study art history in New York, and Balcomb Green provided my major reference for the New York University Institute of Fine Art, where I was accepted. I worked for Sutnar part-time all the time I was at the Institute.

When I went to Italy on a Fulbright grant in 1958, I had been working at *Life* magazine for one year and took a leave of absence from my job, expecting to return there, as it was a good job and gave me time to paint. I could have stayed on. But by then I had been exhibiting at the Tanager Gallery on 10th Street and had also been exhibiting at the Peridot Gallery uptown on Madison Avenue. I had sold a couple of paintings and had also published a couple of articles in the art magazines. While still in Italy with my wife and two-year-old son William, I was offered a teaching job at Pratt Institute, which I accepted. At Pratt, I taught an art history survey course and a course called Art History Studio, as well as Two-Dimensional Design. All of which my background fed into.

At that time — the 1950s and early '60s — it was possible to live in New York on relatively little money. When my G.I. Bill rights came to an end, I was still writing my M.A. thesis, and I wasn't going to be working much, so we were looking for a cheaper place to live. We traded an apartment on 90th Street and Third Avenue that I found with a rent of $75 a month, with Lester Johnson and his wife Josephine, who were looking for a larger apartment, for their apartment on East 4th Street between First Avenue and Avenue A. They had been paying $12 a month, and when we moved there the landlord raised the rent to $17. But then Mr. Sutnar was paying me $1.25 an hour for my work.

George Sugarman in his New York studio, April, 1958

GEORGE SUGARMAN

December 19, 1974

I was born in New York City, out in the Bronx, the South Bronx, the poor part. We moved around a lot. I don't know why. My father couldn't pay the rent half the time. It wasn't so easy for us; there were five children in the family. And I do remember the problem my parents talked about: "Where are we going to get a big, seven-room apartment?"

I think the longest stay we had was somewhere on Prospect Avenue. And for some reason or other, they used to have block parties there, and there was dancing, and I was just an infant. There was a music teacher upstairs who came down and gave us music lessons, and I remember us singing opera. I was very young then. One of my sisters took singing lessons, but she gave us piano lessons. My family was always big on music.

My mother had been a singer, and my father's sisters had been singers in the Oratorio Society. My father wanted to get into vaudeville. The influence of any kind like that was always from my father's side. My mother's family was very vague, I really don't know much about them, strangely enough. There was my father's sister who kept on singing, she had a try at theater . . . you know what I mean.

Literature and music was the main thing. My father was totally uneducated. He hadn't even been through grammar school, but he was always reading, and he talked about writing a book of his memoirs. He was born in Austria, but he came very young. He didn't even speak yet. My mother was born in England, but I think her parents came from Russia and stopped over in England. I know she was born in London. She, too, came over very early, so they were both very American.

So, that block on Prospect Avenue, every now and then — I think it was once a year — had a block party. I remember dancing; they were teaching me the two-step. I remember dancing very early, and the music. We had a gramophone. What were they called? Victrola. In those days you had to wind it up.

And, of course, there was always a lot of singing of serious music in my house. My aunts and my mother had been in the Oratorio Society, so there was always Bach, [Handel's] *Messiah*, and all that. By the time I was in my teen age, I didn't want to hear a female voice for the rest of my life — I hated it! It was all part of being rebellious. Now, I'm going back to it strong in the last four or five years. I remember it took me years to get over the sound of a female voice — not a pop singer, a serious opera singer — even after the rebellion.

That was the art in my life. It was not visual, but I was always interested in that. As soon as I had the nickel for the subway in those days, I discovered the Metropolitan Museum by myself. This was when I was still young, and that continued.

Before the Depression, my father worked for himself. He was a salesman during the 1920s. He used to buy oriental rugs, and he'd pack them and go all over the countryside and sell them. I still remember some of the oriental rugs. They remain in my mind — the glow of them — particularly a purple one. These things were good rugs. They used to wash some of the rugs with an acid to give it a shine like very, very old rugs. The rugs were very attractive, and they sold, but they were genuine rugs. I remember helping him pack them. I loved that part of it. Later, when I got old enough — I guess in my teens and older — I used to go around with him during Christmas, school holidays, and summers, because he wanted someone to help him. So, I saw quite a lot of the country when I was young. They're very heavy, and I was the laborer. We went by car all over New York State, quite far down south, east of St. Louis. That was a very important part of my life. He never could hold a job. Never. He used to reminisce occasionally about a couple of jobs he'd had. He was always getting fired. The continual fights he had with my mother were because he wanted her to go with him, because he felt lonely. She didn't want to because who was going to take care of the kids?

Actually, when we got older, she did occasionally. She never liked it. This went on until the Depression hit, and he started to sell less. He started to sell imitation rugs. The Depression just about killed him. He couldn't make an independent living. And then my sisters, who were ready to become teachers, supported him.

I have three older sisters and a younger brother. I was the older of the two youngest. The sisters became teachers. My oldest sister always wanted to be a teacher. I remember one of her private games was to get out all the books in the house and put them on the bed, because that was the biggest expanse that was available, and they were pupils of hers and she'd teach them. She was always happy as a teacher. She loved it.

None of us were really like our parents. It took us a long time to appreciate them, especially how much my father gave me in terms of the driving and the interest in his wide range of cultural activities. My mother was not passive, because she was the one who held the family together while he was out, but my memories of her were scrubbing and cooking. There were five kids, and we had our squabbles, but we always remained very friendly, helping each other out. We keep in touch, though we're not close anymore — our lives are so different.

After Prospect Avenue we moved to 167th Street, and that's what I really remember, because we lived there a long time, and I had what I consider my childhood friends on that street. It was a gang, and it wasn't. It wasn't a bad gang, it was just the kids on the block. And we kind of formed a baseball team and a football team. This was still grammar school.

By the time I hit high school, I was already becoming an intellectual. I remember in my first year in high school, I was on the track team. I was always a very fast runner. That was my sport. And then I became intellectual. I said, "Why should I waste my time practicing?" There was a group of friends I met in high school, and we were all involved in the arts, literature, and we used to discover and do a lot of things together. I was writing some. You know, it was awful. It took me a while to realize how bad it was.

I was always more interested in the theater and doing stage design. And with this group of friends, we used to read plays and act around a little bit, and I did get into some amateur theater. As a matter of fact, after college, I joined a non-professional left-wing theater that was kind of sponsored by the Group Theater. The Group Theater people used to come down and teach us the Stanislavsky method. They used to go away for the summer and take one of the Catskill Mountain places. It was during the Depression, so it was easy to rent one of those. I got a job a couple of summers in one of those places. All of the waiters were mostly like me, and they let us go to rehearsals and the acts. It was all very romantic, because they were big figures: John Garfield, Clifford Odets, Elia Kazan.

When I went to City College, I majored in literature. I took a couple of art courses. There was a teacher of some kind, an elderly man who wandered around. The classes were upstairs in an attic filled with plaster casts of Greek sculpture. It was lovely. There was no instruction as far as I can remember. Absolutely none. I just sat, and I sketched from the plaster models and ate lunch and read and spent afternoons there. It was pleasant, and I was interested in art. I didn't learn anything.

I hated school. I kept dropping out. It was during the Depression, and the family would support me as long as I was in school, so I stayed in school. I took all the easy courses except the philosophy course I took with Morris Raphael Cohen. He scared me he was so brilliant. And I admired him. He really did a lot for me. He cured my arrogance, thinking that I was an intellectual. And I took some courses from his young assistants. Cohen was very famous in philosophical circles as a logician.

I remember one of his students, Abraham Edel. I took his philosophy courses, and he always surprised me because he gave me As and B-plusses. He restored a little bit of the ego Cohen destroyed. I don't remember many teachers, but I remember them and one or two English teachers. I took some ancient Greek. I just wanted to know the sound of it.

Everyone else — I shouldn't say everyone — was trying to get their teacher's licenses, and I refused. I said I would never be a teacher. I took almost everything. I wasn't very good at math, but I got by, mostly by gypping on the tests. I had no use for honesty. I felt if they forced me to take mathematics, I defended myself. It was a defense. They were attacking me by forcing me. But that was the only course that gave me trouble. It was a very easy school, I thought, even though it was supposed to be so tough. I don't remember, but I must have been getting decent marks, because I kept going back, and they kept letting me go back.

Of course, it was a big political thing then, a very left-wing school. I remember the demonstrations. There was a famous, silly incident in which a resident of the college attacked the picket line with his umbrella. I don't even remember the guy's name. I was involved in that some. And also in some literary clubs.

I used to see my old group that I met in high school; we went to the theater an awful lot. It was practically all Broadway. There was a little bit of Off-Broadway down in the Village, Provincetown Playhouse. But Broadway was very cheap then. You could get a seat for a quarter, always the top row in the top balcony. I saw practically everything. I saw every big star of that time. I even saw Eddie Cantor in *Whoopee*. I think that was the only Ziegfeld Follies I ever saw. I decided I finally might as well see some musicals. I think I saw everything, because at that time I thought even bad theater was important to me, so I could make up my mind about what I thought was bad and good.

I saw Martha Graham. At the very beginning she did solo dancing. I remember going to see her. She gave a performance in Brooklyn in the Brooklyn Academy or, what is it now? The Brooklyn Academy of Music. It was a Saturday matinee, and the theater was filled with women who were tittering, laughing, and all that, and I just fell in love with her. I saw all her performances in New York after that. It was mostly Martha Graham, even though there were a few others. Tamara and her husband [Addison Fowler and Florenz Tamara] were dancing. It was only after the war that the dance flourished.

I liked chamber music, and there was comparatively little chamber music compared to now. You can't possibly go to all of them. We listened to Bing Crosby and Rudy Vallée. Good lord — I do remember sitting in front of a radio listening. There was some jazz at the clubs, but it was expensive. I'm talking now of the Depression. I'm sure there was music being played in basements in Harlem, but I wasn't aware of that in the Depression. I went to the Apollo occasionally. Of course, there was Benny Goodman, but the non-commercial jazz was not available to me. I can't remember if I was interested. I don't think I even knew about it. Somebody who was especially interested in jazz might have known about places, but I didn't.

There was no interest in the family at all in terms of visual art. But I was always drawing and scribbling without it meaning anything. There was no tradition except for literature and music. I remained that way, interested in things other than visual art, and I got a job after the Depression in the WPA like everybody else.

I had a variety of jobs with the WPA. I was doing research. The Museum of Costume Art at that time had some small offices, and I spent most of my time in the library of the Museum of Modern Art. I remember Zero Mostel had some kind of WPA job, too. We became quite friendly. He was an aspiring artist. He was very funny. I think he secretly left his notebooks behind, hoping someone would look at them and they'd be discovered. He may not still paint at this moment, but he did continue to paint for a long time.

I didn't become an artist until very, very late. I got these jobs on the WPA, and I continued to go to the theater a lot, until the war came. And then after the war, before I went back to my job, I knew a woman whose husband was a great yachtsman. He wanted to buy a yacht, and I went into partnership with him. It was beautiful, fantastic. It was a fifty-four-foot schooner, and we took it through the Great Lakes, down the Mississippi, across the Gulf and up the Atlantic to New York. And we were going into business to charter it.

He was a great yachtsman at sea, but the Mississippi River was different. He didn't have the experience. Ordinarily, the routes are called charts, but for the Mississippi you don't get charts, you get maps. It's just like going down the road, because the river shifts every day, and the sand banks are treacherous. We got hung up a couple of times and needed repairs. It took us quite a while to get back to New York. And when we did, his wife said, "That's it. I'm not going to have you go out and charter while I'm home all alone!" We were away quite awhile, but that was a great experience.

I went back to my job, but I wanted to get rid of it. Then I began to draw more and more by myself. I also went to a shrink at that time, and that liberated me a lot. I remember breaking off after two years. I felt that that was enough. I was continuing to draw, but then it became totally compulsive. I kept my job and drew every spare minute. I'd go in the subway and draw. I'd go to movies and draw — I'd draw the backs of people's heads totally compulsively.

And I started to do big imaginary portraits in colored inks. I went to the Museum of Modern Art school for a few months, and then I realized that was it. I had never done anything that was so obsessive. I decided, "What have I got to lose?" I still had the G.I. Bill of Rights, so I quit everything and went over to Paris. And that was the beginning. I was thirty-nine.

I went to Paris by boat. I wouldn't think of going any other way. I took a lot of luggage — all my clothing, which I never used. I had no idea. Just as I had no idea of whom to study with. Before you go, you have to fill out forms for the school you're going to go to. I also took a brush-up course in French, which I continued reading, but I never did speak it. It was a great help. By the time I got through, I was pretty good at speaking French. I just decided that I'd go to [Ossip] Zadkine's — not that I wanted to do sculpture — because I knew his name, and I had seen some of his work here. I didn't terribly like it, but I thought at least he was one of the older men and he'd be an interesting personality.

I didn't know about Léger's school. Or it may also have been that I didn't like Léger's work until much later. It took me a while to see Léger. But I knew Zadkine's name, and I figured once I got there, I could switch schools. I did go there for a year, and then I switched to an academy right across the street from the hotel I was living at, where they left me entirely alone.

Zadkine was a pest. He was nasty, but he was good in certain ways. He was very nervous. He was a high-energy man, and he could be very destructive. After a while, I found I wasn't getting anything out of him, and I covered up my work and didn't let him see it. There was a big piece I worked on. I remember starting in clay, because that's all there was to work with. It was going to be a big farmhouse or some kind of scene in clay. I had all these spatial ideas, and I had no idea what anything was about, and Zadkine was the last person in the world to help me on it. He had no idea what I was trying to do. Basically, he was a very traditional sculptor, modernistic. We also had a model in class, and we worked from her in pen and ink.

So, there was this big expanse of clay, which I flattened out. There was a fence and there was going to be the farmhouse, and I don't know how it evolved, but at the end of six months, it was a family group. I refused to show him anything but the work from the model. The drawing was a big help. I had a lot of trouble making heads, and he kept saying, "If it weren't for your drawing, Sugarman, I'd ask you to leave the school." I couldn't draw heads.

I finally got hold of a skull. I could get a likeness, but I couldn't get the anatomy. So I worked on that. Then I had done a bust, life-size, and I cast it in plaster. And there was a foundry by the name of Sousa. He used to go around, and he put some things of students and unknown artists in bronze, to encourage business, and he put that one of mine in bronze. It was an awful piece. It was modernistic. I've got it buried somewhere, but I'd like to melt it down.

Just before I was ready to leave the school, Zadkine asked if he could see the covered piece. So I showed him, and he looked at it, and he said, "All I can say is I don't understand this sculpture." I took that as a compliment. And I went to the Academy of the Grande Chaumière. They allowed the Americans free range. I met Earl Kerkam there, and we worked in a big studio with all the other Americans.

Then, after a while, I got this little studio of my own, which shows how well you could manage on that little money they gave. It was very cheap. It was just one of these sheds they had in the courtyard. It had been used by an old Italian plaster caster. It was tiny, but it was enough for me. He was retired and lonely, so we talked. He still regarded himself as an Italian even though he'd come to Paris when he was ten years old. His French was perfect, even though he wasn't educated. I remember him using the imperfect subjunctive, which nobody used anymore. And he reminisced. He had worked on Rodins and other very famous artists. I kept that shack until I left. It was just a few francs a month.

During that time, I bought wood and a good set of carving tools, and I started to carve wood. I learned by myself. I bought a welding set and learned how to weld. I sent home for a dollar Arco welding book. And with the help of one Japanese-American, whose name I forget, who told me how to turn on the bottles, I learned how. I did quite a lot of work. I was there four years. From 1951 to 1955.

I had the same experience that most American artists had in Paris. We were shocked at the level of French art. Paris was still the thing in those days. Of course, I knew very little, or my opinions now are very different, but the impression remains that the level of French art was pretty shocking. But I participated as much as I could. There were always these big salons at the end of the year, and as soon as I had something, I was in one. They would take anybody. I was not a full participant in the scene, but the only art being done was by Americans.

I did go to French artists' studios. My French was very good, because for almost two years I deliberately cultivated French friends. And then after that I started to hang around the cafes where the Americans were. So I did meet a lot of French artists, but none of them became well known. We were all horribly shocked and realized we had to come back. That's why I came back.

I was so well adjusted to France, had so many friends, and spoke the language so well that I thought of staying, but I realized it would be artistic suicide. I had met Al Held and got to know him there and knew Sam Francis slightly. I became more friendly with Sam Francis when he got back to the United States. I remember his shows. He was already very well known. He had his group of admirers. He was a great hero to Al Held at that time. He was very helpful to Al. And he was very helpful to me, too, because much later, in the States, he sent a lot of Swiss people around, and through them some dealers got interested in us, and they gave me and Al our first shows in Europe. What I'm saying is it was through Sam.

When I got back to New York, it was totally different from Paris. And of course, temperamentally, being a hysterical New York type, it was suited to me.

AFTERWORD

Here these stories end, tantalizingly — as we know, or should know, that all these artists have gone on to fascinating careers and lives. The next chapter would be their lives and experiences in the 1950s as part of Manhattan's 10th Street gallery scene, where all of these artists showed. That chapter would be followed by their eventual branchings out and discoveries in the diverse artistic ferment of the 1960s, '70s, and beyond.

Some of these artists are no longer with us. Some are still very active today. These previously unpublished memories present surprising details of each artist's upbringing and introduction to the arts. Particularly remarkable is the resilience of each artist as he or she marked out a pathway where none was given. Art schools did exist, but art was not considered, in those days, a reasonable way to make a living, and there could have been little encouragement from parents — even from those who were familiar with the arts.

In some cases, the parents came from worlds vastly different from those in which their children found themselves. They could offer little advice or guidance to a child or young adult who might have artistic aspirations. In several cases, the parents came from Europe, which in those days meant they came from cultures so different from the America of the 1930s and '40s that, again, they would be at a loss to offer much assistance.

These artists found their own paths, and these stories flesh out their beginnings in ways that would have been lost to us had Ada Katz not interviewed them in the mid-1970s. Scholars and others interested in the history of art — and in how someone becomes an artist — will find these documents of considerable value. We at Libellum are glad to be able to bring them into print now for the first time. We are grateful for the collaboration of the Colby College Museum of Art and the support and encouragement of its director, Sharon Corwin.

Vincent Katz

Ronald Bladen (1918–1988) was educated at Emily Carr University of Art and Design and the California School of Fine Arts (later renamed the San Francisco Art Institute). He was a founding member of the cooperative Brata Gallery in 1957. His work was included in the "Primary Structures" exhibition at the Jewish Museum in 1966. He received many commissions for his large-scale minimalist sculptures and exhibited widely during his lifetime.

Lois Dodd (1927–) attended Cooper Union in New York and was one of the co-founders of the cooperative Tanager Gallery in 1952. She taught at Brooklyn College and served on the board of governors of the Skowhegan School of Painting and Sculpture in Maine. She is a member of the American Academy of Arts and Letters and the recipient of the 2005 Augustus Saint-Gaudens Award from Cooper Union. A retrospective of her work was organized by the Kemper Museum in 2012 and traveled to the Portland Museum of Art in 2013.

Sally Hazelet Drummond (1924–) attended Rollins College, Columbia University, the Institute of Design, Chicago, and the University of Louisville. She was a member of the Tanager Gallery. Her work is in the collections of the Museum of Modern Art, the Hirshhorn Museum, the Whitney Museum of American Art, and the Metropolitan Museum. She has received a Fulbright Scholarship and a Guggenheim Fellowship. In 1972, the Corcoran Gallery of Art presented a retrospective exhibition of her work.

Al Held (1928–2005) studied at the Art Students League and the Académie de la Grande Chaumière in Paris. He was a founding member of the Brata Gallery in 1957. He has been the subject of exhibitions at the San Francisco Museum of Modern Art, the Corcoran Gallery of Art, the Institute of Contemporary Art, Philadelphia, and the Contemporary Arts Museum Houston. In 1974, he had a mid-career retrospective at the Whitney Museum of American Art. A traveling exhibition of his late, large-scale works was organized in 2002.

Alex Katz (1927-) attended Cooper Union and the Skowhegan School of Painting and Sculpture and was a member of the Tanager Gallery. The subject of numerous museum exhibitions worldwide, Katz has also collaborated with many poets, including John Ashbery, Kenneth Koch, Ron Padgett, Carter Ratcliff, and John Godfrey, and with the choreographer Paul Taylor.

William King (1925-) attended the University of Florida and Cooper Union; upon graduation, he went to Rome on a Fulbright Scholarship. He was a founder of the Tanager Gallery, and he has taught at the Brooklyn Museum Art School, the University of North Carolina, and UC Berkeley. He is a member of the American Academy of Arts and Letters and was president of the National Academy of Design. He has received numerous awards, including an Honorary Doctorate for Outstanding Achievement in Sculpture from the San Francisco Art Institute.

Phillip Pearlstein (1924-) attended the Carnegie Institute of Technology and New York University's Institute of Fine Arts, from which he received an M.A. in Art History with a thesis on Francis Picabia. He was a member of the Tanager Gallery. He received a Fulbright Scholarship to study in Italy and later taught at Pratt Institute, Yale, and Brooklyn College. He has served as the President of the American Academy of Arts and Letters. He has exhibited his paintings in numerous gallery and museum exhibitions, including a retrospective organized by the Milwaukee Art Museum in 1983.

George Sugarman (1912-1999) graduated from City College of New York in 1934 and served in the U.S. Navy during World War Two. He studied in Paris on the G.I. Bill with sculptor Ossip Zadkine, returning to New York City in 1955 after an extended stay. He was a founding member of the Brata Gallery in 1957. He showed his work in New York at Fischbach Gallery and Robert Miller Gallery. He executed more than thirty commissions during his career. The Kunstmuseum Basel organized a retrospective of his work in 1969.

Ada Katz was educated at New York University, Brooklyn College, and the University of Maryland. She was a cancer researcher at Sloan-Kettering Institute in New York before retiring to raise her son. Her marriage to Alex Katz enlarged her intellectual life by introducing her to many artists, poets, and dancers. She was a co-founder and producer of Eye and Ear Theater, a company dedicated to producing plays by poets with sets by artists. During its ten-year existence, the theater produced plays by John Ashbery, Edwin Denby, Allen Ginsberg, Eileen Myles, Leslie Scalapino, James Schuyler, and others.

Sharon Corwin received her Ph.D. in the History of Art from the University of California, Berkeley. A scholar of American art with a strong interest in modernism and photography, she joined the Colby College Museum of Art in 2003 and served for three years as the Lunder Curator of American Art before being appointed the Carolyn Muzzy Director and Chief Curator in 2006. She has published essays in various books, including *Alex Katz: Maine/New York* (Charta, 2012) and *American Modern: Documentary Photography by Abbott, Evans, and Bourke-White* (University of California Press, 2010).

Cover

Cover photo by Rudy Burkhardt. The Tanager Gallery as seen from the street, 1950s: Alex Katz at top of stairs; Sally Hazelet on far right in window; Lois Dodd bending over; Lucy Sandler behind her. Tanager Gallery records, Archives of American Art, Smithsonian Institution.

Cover design by Oliver Katz.

Frontispiece

Photo by Rudy Burkhardt. From left to right: Angelo Ippolito, Dorothy Pearlstein, Lois Dodd, Nancy Rudolph, and Salley Hazelet, with a sculpture by Sidney Geist and paintings by Salley Hazelet, Tanager Gallery, New York, c. 1957. Courtesy Alexandre Gallery.

Photo Credits

Cover and frontispiece © The Estate of Rudy Burkhardt; p. 16, © The Estate of Ronald Bladen LLC, courtesy Loretta Howard Gallery, NY; p. 22, courtesy Eli King; p. 32, courtesy Alexandre Gallery, NY; p. 42 Sam Francis © 2014 Al Held Foundation, Inc.; p. 49 Adam Reich, © The Estate of Ronald Bladen LLC/ Licensed by VAGA, New York, NY, courtesy Loretta Howard Gallery, NY; p. 50-51, © Lois Dodd, courtesy Alexandre Gallery, NY; p. 52-53, © Sally Hazelet Drummond, courtesy Alexandre Gallery, NY; p. 53, Private Collection; p. 54, courtesy Robert Miller Gallery; p. 54-55, © 2014 Al Held Foundation, Inc.; p. 56-57, Paul Takeuchi © Alex Katz/Licensed by VAGA, New York, NY; p. 58-59, © William King, courtesy Alexandre Gallery, NY; p. 60-61, courtesy the artist and Betty Cuningham Gallery, NY; p. 62-63, © Arden Sugarman/Licensed by VAGA, New York, NY, courtesy Garth Greenan Gallery; p. 64, © The Estate of Ronald Bladen LLC/Licensed by VAGA, New York, NY, courtesy James and Linda Clark; p. 78 © William King, courtesy the artist and Alexandre Gallery, NY; p. 88 © 2014 The Andy Warhol Foundation for the Visual Arts, Inc./ Artists Rights Society (ARS), New York; p. 102 © Arden Sugarman.

We apologize if, due to reasons wholly beyond our control, some of the photo sources have not been listed.

Special thanks to Ada Katz, Don Leistman, Anna Tome, Sharon Corwin, Loretta Howard, Howard Hurst, Garth Greenan Gallery, Phillipe Alexandre, Marie Evans, Arden Sugarman, James O. Clark, Ramon S. Alcolea, Eli King, Betty Cuningham, Mara Held, Chad Ferber, the Al Held Foundation, the Andy Warhol Foundation, and all of the artists and their estates.

Copyediting by Charles Gute.

Eight Begin was designed by Vincent Katz. It was printed in American Typewriter in an edition of 800, of which 26 are lettered A-Z and signed by the editor.

Libellum books
211 West 19th Street, #5
New York, NY 10011
http://www.vanitasmagazine.net

Colby College Museum of Art
5600 Mayflower Hill
Waterville, ME 04901
Tel. (207) 859-0600
www.colby.edu/museum

© 2014 Libellum books, New York
© The President and Trustees of Colby College
© The authors for their texts

First Edition

All rights reserved
ISBN 0-9752993-9-5
Printed by McNaughton & Gunn, Inc.
Saline, MI

Also published by Libellum

March 18, 2003 by Michael Lally
Arrivederci, Modernismo by Carter Ratcliff
Not Veracruz by Joanne Kyger
Revs Of The Morrow by Ed Sanders
In The Field Where Daffodils Grow by Basil King
Natural Light by Norma Cole
TRANS/VERSIONS by Tom Clark
The New World by Tom Clark

www.vanitasmagazine.net

DATE DUE

Demco